T0246029

Former *Great British Bake Off* contestant Michelle Evans-Fecci grew up on a farm, where she learned the basics of cooking, baking and vegetable growing from her parents.

Michelle was known on the show for her flavoursome, colourful bakes and for championing seasonal, locally sourced and homegrown produce.

She now lives in the beautiful seaside town of Tenby in Pembrokeshire with her husband Ben, their teenage son Alfie, little whippet Rosie, and two cheeky hens.

Since she bought her first recipe book as a child, it has been a lifelong dream of Michelle's to write her own. *The Seasonal Baker* is her first cookbook.

The Seasonal Baker

MICHELLE EVANS-FECCI

———

With photographs by Ben Fecci

ROBINSON

ROBINSON

First published in Great Britain in 2022 by Robinson

10 9 8 7 6 5 4 3 2 1

A CIP catalogue record for this book is available from
the British Library.

ISBN 978-1-47214-662-5

Typeset in Capitolium designed by Gerard Unger
Book designed by Andrew Barron at Thextension

Printed and bound in Great Britain by Bell & Bain Limited

Papers used by Robinson are from well-managed forests
and other responsible sources.

Robinson
An imprint of
Little, Brown Book Group
Carmelite House
50 Victoria Embankment
London EC4Y ODZ

An Hachette UK Company
www.hachette.co.uk
www.littlebrown.co.uk

Cook's notes

1 Always buy the best-quality ingredients you can afford.

2 I always use free-range eggs in my baking. They have a bright yellow/golden yolk which adds colour to sponges and custards.

3 Wash all fruits and vegetables before use to make sure they're clean and to remove bacteria.

4 All lemons, limes and oranges should be unwaxed if zesting. If you can't find unwaxed, run the fruit under hot water and scrub with a clean scourer to remove the waxy layer. Dry with a paper towel.

5 A good set of digital scales is a must. Precision is key, so measuring ingredients carefully is important as poorly measured ingredients can affect the overall consistency or result of your bake.

6 Make sure you prepare your cake tins properly. I often buy parchment paper rounds in different sizes to line my tins and lightly grease with cold butter. This will ensure your cakes come out without sticking.

7 For a clean cut (when cutting cheesecakes, tiffin and brownies) heat a sharp knife by running it under a hot tap then dry with a paper towel to ensure a clean cut. Wipe knife in between each slice with a paper towel.

8 I test cakes with a cocktail stick. If the stick comes out clean when poked in the centre it's ready.

9 Always make sure cakes and bakes are completely cold before decorating.

10 When making a layered cake, always put the final trimmed layer on top upside down as it will have a flatter top to decorate.

11 Pop leftover egg whites in a clean, greaseproof bowl or freezer bag and pop in the freezer to use at a later date. Simply defrost and use.

For Ben and Alfie, my world

Contents

Summer

Autumn

Winter

Introduction

My earliest memory of baking is being stood on a stool with my Mam, in an apron that drowned me, taking everything in with fascination, excitedly waiting to see the end result. Growing up on a farm, I learnt the basics of cooking and baking traditional hearty bakes with my Mam and growing veggies with my Dad.

I've always found growing from seed such a magical and rewarding process. It's relaxing, very easy, cheap and it's fun planning what to plant, watching seedlings grow, harvesting and adding them to everyday cooking and baking. Being sustainable and self-sufficient is something we love as a family.

It was my love and passion for baking that made me apply for *The Great British Bake Off*, a show that I'd watched for years in awe of so many talented bakers. To be chosen to bake in the big white tent was nerve-wracking to say the least, but it was an amazing experience I'll never forget and gave me memories that I will always treasure. The endless baking and intense recipe development made me the baker I am today, as it gave me the confidence to try new flavour combinations, become more adventurous and even gain Star Baker in cake week!

Since saving up my pocket money to buy my first cookbook from the touring bus library that came to my school, it has been a lifelong dream of mine to write my own. I still have that book; it's covered in splatters and held together with tape!

The pages of this book are filled with colourful, flavoursome bakes from my kitchen to yours, for you to enjoy. I hope they will become family favourites in your home as they have in mine. These inspiring creations will keep you baking through the year with the best produce each season has to offer. You can go to your local greengrocer, farmers' market or supermarket to check the array of seasonal produce on offer. Or consider planting your own – whether you have a small plant pot, window box, balcony, raised bed or garden veg patch, we can all grow our own!

So, pop on your apron, get baking and watch your loved ones' faces light up when you give them something that's made with love.

Happy Baking!

Michelle x

SPRING

Spring is my favourite time of the year!
The weather is still a little unpredictable, with the risk of late frost, but it sure is an exciting time for sowing seeds and looking forward to the crops to come. You can't beat homegrown fruit and vegetables, from garden to table in no time at all. It doesn't matter if you have a garden veg patch, a small balcony or even just a plant pot – there's always room for a few seeds!

What to sow and plant

As it's still cold outside, we start by sowing pea shoots and micro greens in old margarine tubs and leave them to germinate on a windowsill that gets plenty of sunlight and warmth. They go into dishes like soup, stir fries and salads to give a real delicious and fresh taste of spring.

Other things you can plant include radish, salad leaves/lettuces, leeks, onions, runner beans, French beans, kale, Swiss chard, beetroot, carrots, squash, courgettes, broad beans, sweetcorn, strawberries, blueberries and gooseberries. These can be grown from seed or bought as plug plants.

Potatoes are so easy, tasty and rewarding to grow. You start with a seed potato that grows in any type of soil – all you need is

approximately 20cm/8in of soil, enough to cover them until they're no longer visible. If you're short on space, they can be planted into reusable planting bags, tubs and containers with tall sides, as well as directly into garden planters or a veg patch. As the potatoes grow, continue to earth up over the green foliage until they reach the top of your container or planter. In a few months you'll have potatoes that also store well.

Among our family's favourites are tomatoes. They can be a little temperamental to grow in a cooler environment, but if you have a sheltered, bright, sunny spot or a greenhouse, you must give them a try. With a huge variety of tomatoes available as seeds or as plants, there's something for everyone. A couple of our favourites are 'Gardener's Delight' and 'Shirley', but if you're after something a little different give 'Indigo Rose' a try. If you're short on space or want to grow in a hanging basket or wall planter, 'Tumbling Tom' is an amazing variety that takes up little space and produces tasty fruits. We often keep tomato seeds, especially when I make the Tomato, Raspberry and Mozzarella Galette in this book, dry them out on some kitchen paper and sow the following year. Tomatoes are great eaten fresh, made into chutneys or cooked in sauces that can be frozen and eaten throughout the year.

I sometimes buy supermarket herbs and vegetables like mint, basil, celery and lettuce, use the tops, keep the roots intact in a glass of water to promote regrowth, and in no time at all you'll have more fresh herbs and veg that you can use as cut and come again.

Not a lot of people know that some flowers are edible. Not only do they look good growing in the garden, but you can add a pop of colour to a lot of bakes! Some of my favourite edible flowers to plant this time of year are violas, calendulas, borage and nasturtiums. If you continually pick them, they will reward you with flowers right through the season.

What to harvest

Don't miss out on broad beans that are available during late winter and early spring.

Blood oranges are available during late winter and early spring. They have a distinctive dark flesh and tangy flavour which are perfect added to bakes or turned into delicious marmalade.

And don't forget about wild garlic. It grows in damp shaded areas during spring. These long, pointed leaves with star-shaped white flowers have a delicate taste and are perfect for flavouring butters or pastas, made into salt or added to savoury dishes.

Blueberry, citrus & white chocolate hot cross bun loaf

YOU WILL NEED A 900G/2 LB LOAF TIN & PIPING BAG

———

A twist on our delicious Easter hot cross buns, this fluffy fruity loaf is perfect eaten freshly baked, or sliced and toasted with lashings of butter for breakfast!

SERVES 12

195ml/7fl oz whole milk
50g/1½oz unsalted butter
450g/1 lb strong white bread flour,
    plus extra for dusting
7g sachet fast-action yeast
1 tsp salt
1½ tsp ground cinnamon
1½ tsp ground mixed spice
50g/1½oz soft brown sugar
1 large egg, beaten
100g/3½oz dried blueberries
60g/2oz mixed peel
50g/1½oz white chocolate drops
Olive oil, for greasing

For the cross
2 tbsp plain flour

For the glaze
3 tbsp caster sugar

Tips
Don't discard any slices of stale loaf; turn them into bread and butter pudding, breadcrumbs or even French toast!

Instead of using a tea towel to cover your rising dough, stretch a shower cap over the bowl.

1 Lightly grease the loaf tin with a little olive oil and line with baking parchment so that it overhangs the edges.

2 Pour the milk into a small saucepan and add the butter. Heat on a medium heat until the butter has melted, then set aside.

3 In a large bowl, mix the flour, yeast, salt, spices and sugar together and make a well in the centre. Add the beaten egg gradually, then add the milk, bringing all the ingredients together with a round-bladed knife until the mixture forms a rough ball. Or you can mix this in a stand mixer using the dough hook.

4 Tip the dough onto your worktop and knead until smooth and elastic. Put it into a large bowl, lightly greased. Cover with a clean damp tea towel and leave for 1½–2 hours to double in size.

5 When dough has risen, tip it onto a lightly floured worktop and shape it into a rough rectangle shape with your hands. Scatter over the blueberries, mixed peel and chocolate drops, then knead the dough to evenly distribute the fruits.

6 Weigh the dough and divide into three equal pieces. Shape each piece into an oblong shape, tucking the seam underneath. Lay the pieces side by side in the tin and cover with a clean damp tea towel for around an hour or until the dough is risen and slowly springs back when you prod it gently.

7 Preheat the oven to 220°C (200°C fan oven) Gas 7.

8 For the cross, mix the flour with enough water to make a thick paste by gradually adding a tablespoon of water at a time. Pop it in a small piping bag and snip off the end. Make one long line running lengthways across the buns, then pipe lines the other way to create a cross on each bun.

9 Bake for 25–30 minutes until golden brown. The loaf should sound hollow when you tap its underside. Remove from oven and, using the overhanging parchment, gently lift the loaf from the tin and place on a cooling rack to cool.

10 For the sugar glaze, mix the sugar with 1 tbsp water and, while the loaf is still warm, brush the sugary mixture all over with a pastry brush. Leave to cool, then slice and enjoy!

Cherry & coconut cheesecake brownies

YOU WILL NEED A 20CM/8IN SQUARE TIN OR BROWNIE TIN

I love brownies – nothing quite says indulgence like dark chocolate and cherries. These flavours remind me of a Black Forest gâteau. This recipe can easily be adapted by using dairy-free chocolate, yoghurt and cream cheese to make them vegan-friendly.

MAKES 16

150g/5oz dark chocolate (chopped)
170g/6oz plain flour
1 tsp baking powder
35g/1oz cocoa powder
180g/6½oz golden caster sugar
230ml/8fl oz coconut milk
   (from refrigerator aisle)
50g/1½oz coconut oil (melted),
   plus extra for greasing
1 tsp vanilla bean paste
40g/1½oz milk chocolate drops

For the cheesecake layer
150g/5oz full fat cream cheese
150g/5oz coconut flavoured yoghurt
30g/1oz icing sugar
1 tsp vanilla bean paste

For the topping
60g/2oz cherry compôte
Desiccated coconut

1 Preheat the oven to 180°C (160°C fan oven) Gas 4. Grease the base and sides of the tin and line with baking parchment.

2 Melt the dark chocolate in a heatproof bowl over a pan of simmering water, making sure the bowl doesn't touch the water. Once melted, leave to cool slightly.

3 Sift the flour, baking powder and cocoa powder into a large bowl, and stir in the sugar, making a well in the centre.

4 Whisk the coconut milk, coconut oil and vanilla together in a jug and pour into the well in the flour mixture. Fold the ingredients together using a spatula, add the cooled melted chocolate and fold the chocolate drops through.

5 Pour the mixture into your prepared tin, reserving 2 tbsp of brownie mixture for later. Level with a spatula.

6 To make the cheesecake layer, mix the cream cheese, yoghurt, icing sugar and vanilla together until smooth, then spread on top of the brownie mixture.

7 Add a splash of boiling water to the reserved brownie mixture to loosen it slightly. Spoon it on top of cheesecake mix, dotting it here and there, dragging a skewer through to marble slightly.

8 Add just over half of the cherry compôte to the top and scatter with desiccated coconut.

9 Bake for 35–45 minutes, until the brownie still has a slight wobble in the centre.

10 Remove from the oven and leave to cool in the tin on a cooling rack. Once cooled, lift the brownie out of the tin using the parchment, dot with the remaining cherry compôte and scatter over more desiccated coconut. Slice into squares or bars.

Tip
It is always best to underbake the brownies as they will firm up as they cool.

Leek & potato soup with mini seeded rolls

LARGE SAUCEPAN WITH A LID & 23CM X 30CM/9IN X 12IN BAKING TIN

––––––––

Using stored and overwintered vegetables from the garden is such a great reward for growing your own. I've used onions, leeks and potatoes harvested from our garden for this light, tasty springtime soup, served alongside crusty seeded bread rolls.

SERVES 4

For the soup

1 onion
3 leeks
2 potatoes (approx. 300g/10½oz)
30g/1oz unsalted butter
800ml/1pt 8fl oz vegetable stock
Salt and pepper, to taste

For the rolls

500g/1 lb 1½oz strong
   white bread flour
2 tsp salt
7g sachet fast-action yeast
300–320ml/11fl oz lukewarm water
Handful of seeds, such as sunflower,
   pumpkin, poppy or linseeds
Olive oil, for greasing

To serve

Swirl of single cream and chives
   (optional)

Tip

Double or triple the amount of ingredients in the soup, let it cool completely, then pour into freezer-safe containers or bags and freeze for up to three months. Perfect for taking to work for a quick and easy lunch, or ready for when you return – just heat it up!

1   For the rolls, place the flour in a bowl and add the salt on one side and yeast on the other, followed by three-quarters of the warm water. Bring the mix together with your fingers, adding the remaining water until you have a rough dough that comes away from the sides of the bowl. Alternatively, this can be done in the bowl of a stand mixer, using the dough hook attachment.

2   Knead the dough on the worktop until it becomes smooth and elastic, then pop into a lightly oiled bowl and cover with a clean damp tea towel and leave to double in size. This can take anything from 30 to 90 minutes depending on the temperature indoors.

3   Meanwhile, for the soup, slice the onions, leeks and potatoes into cubes. Melt the butter in a medium-sized saucepan, then add the vegetables and leave to soften for 4–5 minutes, mixing from time to time. Add the vegetable stock to the pan and leave to simmer for 15–20 minutes with the lid on.

4   Transfer the soup to a blender and blitz until smooth. Set to one side for later.

5   When the dough has proved, weigh it and divide into 12 equal pieces. Place one piece of dough on the worktop, cup your hand over it and rotate your hand, gently pressing onto the dough to form a tight ball. Pop it into a lightly oiled baking tin with the seam at the bottom, and repeat with all the pieces. Cover with a clean damp tea towel until the rolls are puffed up and touching.

6   Preheat the oven to 220°C (200°C fan oven) Gas 7, and place a baking tray in the bottom of the oven to heat up.

7   When rolls are ready, they will slowly spring back when you poke them gently. Brush each roll with a little water and scatter over the seeds. Pour a cup of water into the warmed tray in the oven to create steam – this will make delicious crusty rolls.

8   Bake the rolls for 25–30 minutes until they are golden brown and sound hollow when you tap them underneath.

9   Heat the soup gently, season to taste, and garnish with snipped fresh chives and a swirl of cream. Serve with freshly baked rolls and a chunk of cheese!

Wild garlic & mozzarella tear & share

YOU WILL NEED A 30CM/12IN ROUND CAKE TIN

___

You know spring has arrived when the unmistakable scent of garlic is in the air on your woodland and forest walks. This wild garlic and mozzarella stuffed tear and share has to be one of the best garlic breads you'll ever taste! Soft and chewy dough with a delicious garlic punch – perfect for sharing with family and friends.

MAKES 20 SMALL ROLLS

500g/1 lb 1½oz strong white
    bread flour
1 tsp fine salt
7g fast-action yeast
2 tbsp olive oil, plus extra
    for greasing
300–320ml/11fl oz warm water
120g/4oz salted butter
30g/1oz wild garlic leaves
½ tsp flaked sea salt
125g/4½oz mozzarella ball

Parsley, to decorate

1   Make the dough by putting the flour in a large bowl, adding the salt to one side and the yeast to the other. Add the oil and three-quarters of the water and mix well. Keep adding water until all the dough comes away from the side; you may not need it all depending on the absorbency of your flour. Alternatively, you can use a stand mixer with the dough hook attached. Knead the dough until smooth and elastic then place it in a lightly oiled bowl, cover with a clean damp tea towel and leave to prove for about 1½ hours or until doubled in size.

2   While the dough is proving, soften the butter a little and finely chop the wild garlic leaves. Add the garlic and salt to the butter and mix well.

3   Drain the mozzarella and cut into 20 equal pieces. Lightly grease the tin with a little olive oil.

4   Once the dough has doubled in size, weigh it and divide into 20 pieces. Working with one piece at a time, flatten it into a disc shape and place a piece of mozzarella into the centre. Lift the edges and pinch to seal in the cheese. Shape into a ball and continue with the rest. Place the balls into the tin, leaving a little gap between each one. Prove for a further hour or so, topped with a clean tea towel, until springy to touch.

5   Preheat the oven to 220°C (200°C fan oven) Gas 7.

6   When the rolls have risen, generously brush three-quarters of the garlic butter over the dough and bake for 20–25 minutes until pillowy and a light golden colour.

7   Once baked, remove the tin from the oven and place on a cooling rack to cool a little. Brush over the remaining garlic butter and scatter with a little chopped parsley.

Hot cross bun bread & butter pudding

YOU WILL NEED A 23CM/9IN OVENPROOF BOWL OR BAKING DISH

_____

A spin on the British classic! This is the perfect way to use up leftover Easter buns, using extra fruit, spice, zest and custard for an indulgent and comforting pud!

SERVES 4

4 hot cross buns or 6 slices of
   my Blueberry, Citrus and
   White Chocolate Hot Cross
   Bun Loaf (p.19)
40g/1½oz unsalted butter, plus
   extra for greasing
380ml/13½fl oz milk
230ml/8fl oz double cream
½ tsp ground cinnamon
½ tsp ground mixed spice
3 large eggs
80g/3oz golden caster sugar
1 tsp vanilla bean paste
Zest of 1 orange
30g/1oz sultanas
80g/3oz fresh blueberries

1   Preheat the oven to 190°C (170°C fan oven) Gas 5 and lightly grease a bowl or dish with a little butter.

2   Slice the hot cross buns in half and butter each side generously, then arrange the buns in the bowl or dish and set to one side.

3   Heat the milk, cream and spices in a small saucepan on a low heat and leave to cool slightly.

4   Whisk the eggs, sugar and vanilla together in a large jug and add the orange zest. Gradually add the creamy mixture and whisk well.

5   Pour three-quarters of the mixture on top of the buns and leave to soak for 15–20 minutes.

6   Scatter with the sultanas and blueberries, pushing down slightly, then add the remaining creamy mixture.

7   Bake for 30–40 minutes until golden brown and puffed up.

Apricot & almond flapjacks

YOU WILL NEED A 23CM/9IN SQUARE TIN

These flapjacks are studded with juicy apricots and crunchy nuts and seeds.
The condensed milk adds extra creaminess, taste and texture.
They are the perfect tasty snack and a great addition to any lunchbox.

MAKES 10

150g/5oz unsalted butter
115g/4oz condensed milk
100g/3½oz soft brown sugar
2 tbsp golden syrup
1 tsp vanilla bean paste
70g/2½oz dried apricots
35g/1oz blanched almonds
300g/10½oz porridge oats
30g/1oz mixed seeds (sunflower,
    pumpkin, poppy and linseeds)

1   Preheat oven to 190°C (170°C fan oven) Gas 5 and line the tin with baking paper.

2   Place the butter, condensed milk, sugar, golden syrup and vanilla into a saucepan and heat gently until all the mixture has melted and is smooth.

3   Roughly chop the apricots and almonds and add these to the saucepan (reserving a few for the top) along with the porridge oats and mix well. Scatter in the seeds, roughly mix and pour the mixture into the tin.

4   Press the mixture into the tin with the back of a spoon and scatter the remaining apricots and almonds on top. Bake for 20–25 minutes. This makes a soft chewy flapjack, so bake it a little longer if you prefer yours firmer. Leave to cool in the tin for 10 minutes.

5   Lift the flapjack out of the tin using the baking paper and cut into squares or slices.

Tip
For soft and chewy flapjacks that melt in the mouth, make sure you don't overbake them. They will continue to cook in the residual heat of the tin as they cool and firm up.

Pancakes with maple & peanut butter sauce & sliced bananas

YOU WILL NEED A GRIDDLE PAN/PANCAKE PAN/FRYING PAN

Pancakes don't get much better than this! These light and fluffy pancakes are great for Pancake Day, breakfast or even brunch. The maple and peanut sauce is nutty, sweet and the perfect flavour pairing to sliced banana.

MAKES 12 SMALL PANCAKES

For the pancakes
180g/6½oz plain flour
2 tsp baking powder
2 tbsp caster sugar
Pinch of salt
250ml/9fl oz milk
2 large eggs
4 tbsp sunflower oil, plus
    extra for greasing

**For the maple and
peanut butter sauce**
30g/1oz maple syrup
1½ tbsp peanut butter
¼ tsp vanilla bean paste
Pinch of salt

To serve
Sliced banana
Honey roasted peanuts

1 Put the flour, baking powder, sugar and salt in a large bowl. Make a well in the middle, add the milk, eggs and oil and whisk together gently. Continue whisking until the batter is smooth and lump free, then pour into a jug. Set aside.

2 To make the sauce, mix the maple syrup, peanut butter and vanilla in a small bowl, add a pinch of salt and mix well.

3 Heat a griddle pan, pancake pan or frying pan, and lightly grease with a little oil. Pour a little of the batter mixture (approx. 2 tbsp) onto the pan. Once it's bubbling and golden … flip! Continue until all the batter is used up; you should have around 12 small pancakes. Wrap the pancakes in a clean tea towel to keep warm.

4 Slice the banana and start layering the pancakes on a plate. Top with the sauce, sliced bananas and peanuts.

Bara brith

———

This wonderful, fruity, sticky tea loaf is a huge favourite in our house
and was one of our late Grandad's favourites. It is incredibly simple to make,
bursting with flavour and formed the inspiration for my *Bake Off*
Bara Brith that won me Star Baker in cake week.

SERVES 10

300ml/11fl oz strong tea
  (made with 6 tea bags)
150g/5oz currants
150g/5oz sultanas
45g/1½oz dried cranberries
230g/8oz light muscovado sugar
285g/10oz self-raising flour
1 large egg, beaten
1½ tbsp honey
Butter, for greasing

1 Boil the kettle and make a jug of tea using the teabags.
Leave it to brew for about 10 minutes.

2 Put the dried fruits and sugar in a bowl along with the hot tea.
Cover with a clean tea towel and leave overnight for the fruits to
plump up.

3 Lightly grease the loaf tin and line with baking parchment.
Preheat the oven to 170°C (150°C fan oven) Gas 3.

4 Add the flour, beaten egg and honey to the fruit mixture
and mix well with a spatula.

5 Pour the mixture into the tin and level with a spatula.
Bake for 80–90 minutes or until a skewer comes out clean.

6 Leave to cool in the tin for a few minutes, then remove the loaf
from the tin and leave it to cool on a cooling rack.

7 When cold, slice and enjoy with a smear of butter!

Tip
By soaking the dried fruit in tea
overnight, the fruits plump up and
the tea becomes thick and syrupy.

Rainbow chard quinoa crusted quiche

YOU WILL NEED A 20CM/8IN ROUND FLUTED TART TIN

———

We love quiche, and using cooked quinoa instead of pastry as a base
elevates this quiche to the next level. The delicious, crispy, chewy crust
makes a nice change to traditional pastry.

SERVES 6

2 large egg whites
250g/9oz cooked quinoa
400g/14oz rainbow chard
170g/6oz smoked bacon
1 small onion
80g/3oz mature cheese (grated)
2 large eggs
200ml/7fl oz double cream
Salt and pepper, to taste
Oil/butter for greasing

1 Preheat the oven to 200°C (180°C fan oven) Gas 6 and lightly grease the tin.

2 Whisk the two egg whites in a bowl and add the cooked quinoa, reserving a tablespoon of the egg white. Mix together to coat the quinoa, then tip into the tin. Using the back of a spoon, press the quinoa firmly up against the sides and onto the base of the tin. Bake in the oven for 15 minutes until the case is dry to touch and shrinks away from the sides a little. Brush the sides and base with the remaining egg white and pop back into the oven for 5 minutes.

3 For the filling, trim the leaves from the rainbow chard and roughly chop. Steam the chopped leaves and stems for 5–10 minutes to soften and place them on kitchen paper to absorb the moisture.

4 Cube the bacon and finely dice the onion. Gently fry them over a medium heat, then transfer to a bowl to cool using a slotted spoon.

5 Place the cooled bacon, onions and chard leaves into the base of the crust, top with grated cheese, then arrange the chard stems in a circular pattern starting from the outside and working inwards, shaping the chard with your hands as you go.

6 Whisk the two whole eggs with the cream and season with salt and pepper. Fill the tin halfway with the creamy mixture, then transfer it onto the shelf of the oven and fill to the top. Bake for 25–30 minutes until golden with a slight wobble in the centre.

7 Leave to cool in the tin, then transfer to a board or platter and slice.

Orange, almond and maple shortbread

YOU WILL NEED A 20CM/8IN ROUND TART TIN

These orange and almond shortbread biscuits are deliciously light and have a crumbly texture. I press and dry the violas from our garden and gently lay them onto the baked shortbread for a floral springtime touch!

SERVES 8

215g/7½oz soft unsalted butter
100g/3½oz icing sugar
2½ tsp maple syrup
¼ tsp salt
Zest of 2 large oranges
75g/2½oz ground almonds
165g/6oz plain flour
1 tbsp dried calendula petals
    (optional)
Caster sugar, to dust

Dried pressed edible flowers,
    to decorate

1 Beat the butter until light and fluffy, then add the icing sugar and beat well. Add the maple syrup, salt and orange zest, then mix in the ground almonds and flour, and beat until fluffy. Add the dried calendula petals and mix well.

2 Wrap the dough in baking parchment and pop in the fridge for an hour to firm up.

3 Preheat the oven to 190°C (170°C fan oven) Gas 5. Remove the dough from the fridge and place inside the tart tin.

4 Press the dough firmly into the tin using the back of a spoon and prick all over with a fork.

5 Bake for approximately 20 minutes until lightly golden brown. Leave to cool in the tin a little, then place dried edible flowers on top, pressing down gently, and sprinkle with a little caster sugar. Score and slice while the shortbread is still warm, then turn it out onto a cooling rack and leave to cool completely.

Tip
I always press my edible flowers as I hate seeing them go over. Pick the flowers when they are at their best, pat them dry, then press between two sheets of blotting paper or kitchen roll, face down in a heavy book or flower press for around 2 weeks. They need to be dry and papery to touch and all the moisture gone to store.

Granola

YOU WILL NEED A LARGE BAKING SHEET & A LARGE CLEAN JAR WITH A LID

––––––––

Everyone can do with an energy boost from time to time, and this simple-to-make granola offers just that. This recipe is perfect for using up those leftover nuts, dried fruits and seeds that we all have left lying around in our cupboards.

FILLS 1 LARGE GLASS JAR

30g/1oz pistachios
30g/1oz whole almonds
40g/1½oz pecans
30g/1oz walnuts
30g/1oz flaked almonds
20g/½oz chopped hazelnuts
40g/1½oz dried apricots
40g/1½oz dried figs
20g/½oz sultanas
40g/1½oz dried cranberries
60g/2oz dried dates
20g/½oz dried blueberries
100g/3½oz pumpkin seeds, golden
    linseeds, sunflower seeds and
    poppy seeds
30g/1oz dried coconut slices
1½ tsp ground cinnamon
240g/8½oz porridge oats
7 tbsp honey

1 Preheat the oven to 180°C (160°C fan oven) Gas 4.

2 Roughly chop the fruits and nuts then place in a large bowl.

3 Add all the other dry ingredients, drizzle over the honey and mix well.

4 Spread the mixture over a large baking sheet and bake for 20–25 minutes, stirring from time to time.

5 Leave to cool, then transfer to a clean jar.

Tip
This granola is ideal for mixing with yoghurt and milk, or topping cakes, muffins and Bircher (see p.136). You don't have to stick to my quantities above; use any leftover bits of dried fruit and nuts you have to hand.

Vanilla, rhubarb & raspberry celebration cake

YOU WILL NEED 3 X 15CM/6IN ROUND CAKE TINS & A PIPING BAG & ROUND NOZZLE

This vanilla-flavoured celebration cake filled with seasonal rhubarb and raspberry jam is delicious. By adding a floral edible printed wrap, you can make this cake the perfect centrepiece at any celebration or special get-together. I top it with sugarcraft flowers, which I enjoy making in my spare time. They are always a talking point as sometimes it's difficult to tell if they are real or not.

SERVES 8-10

For the cake
350g/12½oz unsalted butter,
   softened, plus extra for greasing
350g/12½oz golden caster sugar
6 large eggs, beaten
350g/12½oz plain flour
½ tsp baking powder
2 tsp vanilla bean paste
3-4 tbsp milk, to loosen

For the buttercream
300g/10½oz unsalted butter,
   softened
600g/1 lb 5oz icing sugar
1 tsp vanilla bean paste
1-2 tbsp milk, to loosen

Rhubarb and Raspberry Jam
(see p.184)

Edible icing sheet (optional)
Sugarcraft flowers, leaves and
   berries (optional)

Tip
Edible icing sheets are available to buy in shops and online. If you want to give sugarcraft a try, there are many online tutorials, books and classes available where you can learn how to make decorations. I find it very relaxing and they look so beautiful added to cakes as decoration.

1 Preheat the oven to 180°C (160°C fan oven) Gas 4. Lightly grease the tins and line the bases with baking parchment.

2 Beat the butter and sugar until pale, light and fluffy.

3 Gradually add half the beaten egg, followed by half the flour and baking powder, mixing well. Then add the remaining egg and flour and mix briefly. Add the vanilla and milk to loosen, mix to combine, then divide the mixture between the tins and bake for 30-40 minutes or until a skewer comes out clean. Leave the sponges to cool slightly then remove from the tins and leave to cool completely on a wire rack.

4 For the buttercream, beat the butter until light and smooth, then add the icing sugar and vanilla and beat well until very light and pale. Add enough milk to loosen, then transfer to a large piping bag fitted with a large round nozzle.

5 Level the cooled cakes by trimming off the domed tops, then, using a sharp knife, cut each in half to give six equal layers.

6 Add a touch of buttercream to a cake stand or cake plate and place one layer of sponge on top. Spread a little buttercream on the sponge with a palette knife, then pipe a ring of buttercream half an inch in around the edge and fill the centre with 2-3 tsp of jam. The buttercream will act like a dam and stop the jam escaping. Continue with the remaining sponges in the same way, finishing off with buttercream only for the very top. Pipe a thin layer of buttercream all around the cake, smoothing with a palette knife to form the crumb coat. Pop into the fridge to firm up.

7 Place the remaining buttercream into a bowl and beat until smooth, then spread it all over the cake and use a cake scraper to smooth the sides and the top.

8 Pop the cake back in the fridge to firm up slightly.

9 If using an edible icing wrap, press this firmly around the sides of the cake and top with sugarcraft flowers, leaves and berries as decoration.

Lemon posset with pistachio & cardamom biscuits

YOU WILL NEED 3–4 RAMEKINS, GLASSES OR TEACUPS, A FOOD PROCESSOR,
A BAKING SHEET & A COOKIE CUTTER

————

My easy citrusy set desserts look super impressive served in cute
little teacups with homemade cardamom and pistachio biscuits – perfect
for dunking into this smooth zingy pud!

SERVES 3–4

For the posset
400ml/14fl oz double cream
100g/3½oz caster sugar
Zest and juice of 1 lemon

For the biscuits
3 cardamom pods (seeds removed)
35g/1oz pistachios
100g/3½oz icing sugar
200g/7oz plain flour
½ tsp vanilla bean paste
100g/3½oz unsalted butter, softened
1 egg yolk

1   To make the biscuits, whizz the cardamom pods and pistachios in a food processor until fine, then add the icing sugar and flour and whizz together. Add the vanilla, butter and egg yolk and whizz until the dough comes together. Flatten the dough into a disc shape, wrap in baking parchment and pop it into the fridge to firm up for around 30 minutes.

2   Meanwhile, for the posset, heat the double cream and sugar in a saucepan over a low heat until the sugar dissolves. Turn the heat up, bring to the boil and leave to cool. Once cooled, add the lemon juice and zest and divide between the ramekins, glasses or teacups. Pop them into the fridge to set.

3   Preheat the oven to 180°C (160°C fan oven) Gas 4 and line a baking sheet with a silicon mat or baking parchment.

4   Remove the chilled dough from the fridge and roll out on a lightly floured surface to approximately 6mm thick. Stamp out biscuits with a cookie cutter in the shape of your choice.

5   Bake the biscuits for 10–12 minutes or until the edges are starting to change to a light golden colour. Remove from the oven and leave to harden for a few minutes on the baking sheet, then transfer to a cooling rack to cool completely.

6   Remove the posset from the fridge and enjoy with a biscuit or two.

Bacon, cheese & chive soda bread

YOU WILL NEED A FRYING PAN & A BAKING SHEET

This loaf is the quickest and easiest you'll ever make, all done in one bowl, so there's hardly any washing up! Using chives and flowers from our garden adds a delicate, flavourful and aromatic whisper to this loaf. It is so delicious!

SERVES 8

3 slices of smoked bacon
200g/7oz plain flour
200g/7oz wholemeal flour
Salt and pepper
100g/3½oz mature cheese, grated
Small bunch of fresh chives,
    roughly chopped
Chive flowers (optional)
1 tsp bicarbonate of soda
300ml/11fl oz buttermilk

1   Preheat oven to 220°C (200°C fan oven) Gas 7.

2   Finely chop the bacon and fry in a frying pan on a medium heat, then use a slotted spoon to transfer it to a plate to cool.

3   Put the flours, and a little salt and pepper, into a large bowl, then add the cooled bacon, cheese and herbs along with the chive flowers, if using, and roughly mix. Stir in the bicarbonate of soda and mix.

4   Add the buttermilk, then, working quickly, bring the dough together. Tip it out onto the worktop and shape into a circular shape.

5   Lift the dough onto a baking sheet and flatten slightly. Then, using a sharp knife, make a cross on the top, cutting almost all the way down to the base and easing the sides apart slightly with the knife.

6   Bake for 25–30 minutes until golden brown. The loaf should sound hollow when you tap the base.

Tips
Best eaten on the day but great toasted too!

If you can't get hold of buttermilk, add 1 tbsp of lemon juice to whole milk and leave it for 5–10 minutes to curdle.

Blood orange crème brûlée with rosemary-infused sugar

YOU WILL NEED 4–5 RAMEKINS, A DEEP BAKING TRAY & A BLOWTORCH (OPTIONAL)

The best part of eating this dessert is gently tapping the crunchy caramelised rosemary top to reveal the tart, zingy, rich and creamy baked orange custard underneath. Make the most of these red-fleshed oranges when they come into season.

SERVES 4–5

330ml/11½fl oz double cream
1 tsp vanilla bean paste
Zest of two blood oranges,
   juice of one
4 egg yolks
70g/2½oz rosemary-infused caster
   sugar (plus extra for top)

1 Preheat oven to 170°C (150°C fan oven) Gas 3.

2 Pour the cream and vanilla into a small saucepan and add the zest of two oranges. Heat gently and allow to come to a simmer. Remove from the heat and set to one side.

3 Whisk the egg yolks in a medium-sized bowl along with the sugar until pale and light. Add the juice of one orange, then gradually add the warm cream mixture little by little, scraping the vanilla flecks out of the pan and continuing to whisk until smooth.

4 Strain the mixture through a fine sieve into a jug, encouraging the vanilla seeds through.

5 Depending on their size, place four or five ramekins into a deep baking tray and fill each ramekin.

6 Fill the baking tray with warm water until it reaches three-quarters of the way up the sides of the ramekins.

7 Bake for 25–30 minutes until just set with a wobble in the centre.

8 Once baked, remove the ramekins from the tray and leave to cool on a cooling rack. Pop the ramekins in the fridge until ready to eat, or overnight.

9 Just before serving, remove the ramekins from the fridge and scatter the extra sugar on top of each one, using the back of a spoon to spread the sugar to completely cover them.

10 Lightly spray the tops with water to dampen the sugar and use a blowtorch to caramelise the sugar, or pop the ramekins under a hot grill, but be careful not to burn them!

Tip
To make rosemary sugar, chop 2–3 sprigs of fresh rosemary and place in a clean jar, then top up with caster sugar and shake to mix. The flavour will infuse within a week or so.

Truffle, garlic & rosemary focaccia

YOU WILL NEED A 23 X 30CM/9IN X 12IN BAKING TIN

My rosemary and Parmesan-flecked focaccia bread, dotted with
caramelised garlic, is heavenly. The added truffle oil gives it an intense garlicky,
earthy aroma and was inspired by the flavours of the truffle oil and
Parmesan chips I love from a well-known restaurant chain!

SERVES 12

500g/1 lb 1½oz strong white
  bread flour
2 tsp fine salt
7g sachet fast-action yeast
2 tbsp olive oil, plus extra for
  greasing
350–380ml/12½–13½fl oz
  lukewarm water
3 tbsp white truffle oil
4–5 garlic cloves, sliced
2–3 sprigs of fresh rosemary
30g/1oz Parmesan, grated, plus
  a little extra to finish
1 tsp flaky sea salt/truffle salt

1 Place the flour in a large bowl, add the salt on one side and
the yeast on the other, then add the olive oil and three-quarters
of the water. Mix well, continuing to add the remaining water
until the dough comes together and away from the sides of the
bowl. The dough will be stretchy and slightly sticky. Depending
on the absorbency of your flour, you may not need all the water.
Alternatively, you can make this in the bowl of a stand mixer
with the dough hook attached.

2 Turn the dough onto your worktop and knead until smooth.
Lightly oil a large bowl and pop the dough inside, covering it with
a clean damp tea towel. Leave it for around an hour to double
in size.

3 When the dough is ready, tip it onto the worktop and stretch it
into a rough rectangular shape. Oil the tin and lift the dough into
it, stretching it into the corners and encouraging it to stay. Cover
the dough again and leave for about 45–60 minutes to prove.

4 Preheat the oven to 220°C (200°C fan oven) Gas 7. Mix 1 tbsp
truffle oil with 1 tbsp water and set aside.

5 Once the dough is ready – it should spring back when you poke
it – press your fingers into the dough to make deep dimples and
drizzle over the reserved oil mixture.

6 Push pieces of garlic and rosemary into the dimples randomly,
then scatter over the grated Parmesan and the salt.

7 Bake for 20–25 minutes until golden brown.

8 Drizzle over the remaining 2 tbsp of truffle oil and a little
extra grated Parmesan.

9 Leave to cool on a wire rack, then slice and enjoy!

Coffee & walnut cupcakes

YOU WILL NEED A 12-HOLE CUPCAKE TIN & PAPER CASES, PIPING BAG & NOZZLE

———

These deliciously light coffee-flavoured cupcakes, studded with nuts and topped with thick, sweet frosting, have become a firm favourite with my family and friends alike. They are the ideal sweet treat!

MAKES 12

For the cupcakes
180g/6½oz unsalted butter
180g/6½oz golden caster sugar
3 large eggs, beaten
180g/6½oz plain flour
1 tsp baking powder
¼ tsp bicarbonate of soda
3 tsp instant coffee mixed with
    1½ tbsp boiling water, cooled
60g/2oz walnuts, finely chopped

For the coffee buttercream
180g/6½oz unsalted butter, softened
360g/12½oz icing sugar
5 tsp instant coffee mixed with
    1 tbsp boiling water, cooled

12 walnut halves, to decorate

1 Preheat the oven to 180°C (160°C fan oven) Gas 4 and line the cupcake tin with 12 paper cases.

2 Beat the butter and sugar together in a large bowl until light and fluffy, then add half the beaten eggs, half the flour, the baking powder and bicarbonate of soda and mix well. Add the remaining beaten egg and flour and the cooled coffee. Fold through the chopped nuts and evenly fill the paper cases until they are three-quarters full.

3 Bake the cupcakes for 20 minutes until nicely risen or until a skewer comes out clean when poked in the middle.

4 Remove the cupcakes from the tin and leave them to cool on a cooling rack.

5 Meanwhile, make the coffee-flavoured buttercream. Beat the softened butter until light and pale in a bowl with a wooden spoon, an electric hand whisk or a stand mixer, then add the icing sugar in two stages. Scrape the bottom and sides of the bowl to make sure the buttercream is evenly mixed through.

6 Add the cooled coffee a teaspoon at a time, mixing well in between each addition. Depending on your individual taste, you may not want to add all the coffee so taste as you go. Beat until the buttercream is smooth and pop into a piping bag fitted with a nozzle of your choice. (I use an ice cream swirl nozzle for these.)

7 When the cupcakes are completely cooled, pipe the coffee buttercream on top and decorate each cupcake with a walnut half or a sprinkling of chopped walnuts.

Tip
These cupcakes can be made with or without nuts.

SUMMER

Come summer, once the worry of late frost
has passed, all plants can be sown or planted straight outside.
It's good to plan ahead and think of the crops that can keep you
going right through into next year. With warmer weather plants
thrive and some are ready to harvest within just a few weeks.

What to plant

Now is the time to plant out your runner beans, mangetout, broad beans and peas. Make sure you train the climbers onto a support frame as they'll grow amazingly well with the help of bamboo sticks, against a trellis or even up string. Keep picking them and the plants will produce more and more; nothing beats the taste of freshly picked garden peas.

There are so many things you plant out this time of year, such as summer lettuce, spring onions, turnips, herbs, carrots, pumpkins, squash, courgette and cucumbers. The key to growing through the season is successional sowing, so keep sowing every 2 to 4 weeks to keep your crops coming to harvest later in the year.

What to harvest

Fruits and vegetables grow so well in the warmth of the summer months, so there is plenty to harvest this time of year. All the hard work in spring is starting to pay off and you'll soon be rewarded with lots of fresh produce. Harvest the outer leaves of Swiss chard, young beetroot leaves, spinach, pea shoots, lettuce, broad beans and micro greens, along with crunchy radishes and small beetroots. Other summer crops to harvest include runner beans, courgettes and carrots. From mid-summer you'll be able to start harvesting cucumbers, delicious tomatoes and potatoes, followed by sweetcorn later in the season.

As well as fresh vegetables, throughout the summer season the garden will also be producing an abundance of beautiful fruit. Warm, ripe strawberries picked and eaten on the same day are an absolute delight, while other fruits to harvest include blueberries, rhubarb, gooseberries and raspberries. Fruit harvested from your own garden is packed with stunning flavour, the like of which you may not have tasted before.

While it's always a gardener's perk to eat the fresh fruit when it's picked, there are other ways we can use it. I love to make jams, chutneys and curds with what I harvest and even freeze a lot to give us seasonal fruits to eat throughout the year. Later on in the book (p.180), I'll share with you some of my favourite preserving recipes.

Tip

When harvesting carrots, don't throw away the tops. They are perfect for making pesto which can be frozen into ice-cube trays and used to stir through pasta, to have with fish or even my Carrot-Top Pesto Oven-Baked Sandwich (p.117).

Lemon verbena loaf cake

YOU WILL NEED A 900G/2 LB LOAF TIN

This light, zingy cake with delightful fragrant lemon verbena is perfect served as a teatime treat. Adding the drizzle while the cake is still warm helps it soak right through, ensuring it stays nice and moist.

SERVES 12

For the loaf cake
230g/8oz unsalted butter,
    plus extra for greasing
230g/8oz lemon verbena-infused
    caster sugar
4 medium eggs, beaten
230g/8oz plain flour
1 tsp baking powder
Zest of 2 lemons
4 tbsp orange calendula petals

For the drizzle
Juice of 1 lemon
60g/2oz lemon verbena-infused
    caster sugar

For the icing
3–4 tsp lemon juice
100g/3½oz icing sugar

Edible flowers, to decorate
    (optional)

1 Preheat your oven to 180°C (160°C fan oven) Gas 4. Grease the loaf tin and line it with baking parchment.

2 Beat the butter and sugar together until light and fluffy, then add half of the beaten egg, then half of the flour and mix well. Add the baking powder, then the remaining egg and flour and mix well.

3 Add the zest of the lemons and the flower petals and briefly mix. Pour the mixture into the prepared tin and bake for 40–50 minutes until lightly golden or until a skewer comes out clean, then place the tin onto a cooling rack.

4 To make the drizzle, simply mix the lemon juice and sugar in a small bowl. While the cake is still warm, poke a few holes in the top with a skewer and pour over the lemon drizzle. Leave to cool before removing the cake from the tin.

5 Place the cooled cake onto a cake board or plate, and make the icing by mixing lemon juice little by little into the icing sugar to make a thick but runny icing.

6 Spoon the icing over the cake and encourage it to drip slightly over the edges. Decorate with edible flowers.

Tip
I love infusing sugar with herbs! For this recipe I chopped ten leaves from the lemon verbena growing in my garden, mixed them with caster sugar and left to infuse for a couple of weeks. Lemon verbena gives the sugar a citrusy aroma; it's refreshingly lemony and perfect for adding to bakes and sweet treats. It is a perennial herb that comes back year after year and when picked fresh stores amazingly well.

Rhubarb, blueberry & lemon crumble top muffins

YOU WILL NEED A 12-HOLE CUPCAKE TIN & 8 MUFFIN CASES

These buttery, soft and super-light muffins are packed with seasonal fruits and topped with crunchy crumble.

MAKES 8 LARGE MUFFINS OR
12 SMALLER ONES

For the muffins
130ml/4½fl oz buttermilk
30ml/1fl oz vegetable oil
1 large egg
1 tsp vanilla bean paste
220g/7½oz plain flour
1 tsp baking powder
1 tsp bicarbonate of soda
160g/5½oz golden caster sugar
Zest of 1 lemon
100g/3½oz rhubarb, diced
80g/3oz blueberries
1 tbsp poppy seeds

For the crumble top
40g/1½oz unsalted butter
40g/1½oz plain flour
40g/1½oz caster sugar
30g porridge oats
Few flaked almonds

1 Preheat the oven to 220°C (200°C fan oven) Gas 7 and add eight muffin cases to the tin (I use large tulip muffin cases).

2 To make the crumble, rub the butter and flour together to create chunky breadcrumbs. Add the sugar and porridge oats and mix well.

3 For the muffins, whisk the buttermilk, oil, egg and vanilla in a jug until smooth.

4 Tip the flour, baking powder, bicarbonate of soda and sugar into a large bowl and mix. Add the lemon zest and toss the diced rhubarb and blueberries in the mix. Add the poppy seeds, then pour the wet ingredients into the bowl and gently mix.

5 Quickly divide the muffin mixture between the cases and top with the crumble. Scatter over a few flaked almonds and bake for 15–20 minutes until lightly golden brown.

Tip
To make this recipe go further, use cupcake cases. The recipe should make 12 regular-sized muffins or eight large ones.

Carrot cake with tahini cream cheese frosting

YOU WILL NEED 2 X 15CM/6IN ROUND CAKE TINS & A PIPING BAG

Velvety tahini cream cheese frosting adds a nutty flavour to my light, spiced carrot cake and complements the spices running through it really well. Perfect as a sweet treat any time of the day! This delicious carrot cake recipe is based on the one Paul and Prue loved in the *Great British Bake Off* tent that helped me get Star Baker in cake week!

SERVES 8–10

For the cake
3 large eggs
240g/8½oz golden caster sugar
225ml/8fl oz vegetable oil,
    plus extra for greasing
200g/7oz carrots, grated
220g/7½oz plain flour
¾ tsp baking powder
¾ tsp bicarbonate of soda
2 tsp ground cinnamon
2 tsp ground mixed spice
60g/2oz sultanas
Zest of 1 large orange
100g/3½oz walnuts,
    roughly chopped

For the tahini cream cheese frosting
160g/5½oz unsalted butter
80g/3oz tahini
180g/6½oz full fat cream cheese
380g/13½oz icing sugar

30g/1oz walnuts, finely chopped,
    to decorate

Tip
No need to peel the carrots, just wash them well and top and tail them, then coarsely grate!

1 Preheat the oven to 190°C (170°C fan oven) Gas 5. Grease the two cake tins and line the bases.

2 In a large bowl, beat the eggs. Add the sugar, oil and carrots and gently mix.

3 Add the flour, baking powder, bicarbonate of soda and spices to the bowl and mix well. Add the sultanas, zest and nuts, mix through and divide the mixture between the two tins equally.

4 Bake for 35–40 minutes or until a skewer comes out clean when poked in the centre.

5 Remove the cakes from the tins and leave to cool on a wire rack. Once completely cooled, level the tops and slice each cake in half.

6 For the frosting, beat the butter until soft, add the tahini and cream cheese and beat well. Add the icing sugar and continue to mix until smooth.

7 To assemble, place a dab of frosting on a cake stand or board, and add one layer of the cake on top. This will help keep the cake in place. Add a couple of spoons of frosting to the top and level with a spatula, then continue layering the remaining sponges on top in the same way.

8 Cover the sides of the cake with the remaining frosting (reserving a little for piping) and smooth with a large palette knife or cake scraper.

9 Pop the remaining frosting in a piping bag with a nozzle of your choice, pipe on top and scatter chopped walnuts around the base and up the sides of the cake.

Rainbow carrot & beetroot tart

YOU WILL NEED A ROASTING TIN & A LARGE BAKING SHEET

This puff pastry tart is packed with flavour and is also vegetarian.
You can either make your own pastry or use ready-rolled puff pastry. By switching
the pastry and cream cheese to dairy-free it can be vegan too! The flaky pastry,
the creaminess of the beetroot cream cheese and the sweet caramelised carrots
are a gorgeous flavour combination. Perfect for slicing and serving
with a side salad as a light and tasty lunch.

SERVES 4

For the pastry
200g/7oz strong white bread flour
1 tsp fine salt
200g/7oz unsalted butter
100ml/3½fl oz cold water

Or 1 sheet of ready-rolled puff pastry

For the filling
8 coloured carrots
4 tbsp honey
2 tbsp balsamic vinegar
100g/3½oz cooked beetroot
180g/6½oz cream cheese
Fresh thyme and rosemary

Tip
Making rough puff pastry from scratch is much quicker than proper puff pastry, but it still takes a lot of hands-on time. It is well worth the effort as it's buttery and flaky, so if you have the time, give it a try! There is no shame in buying a sheet or block of ready-made pastry though. It's readily available from most supermarkets frozen or chilled.

1 To make the pastry, sift the flour into a large bowl with the salt. Roughly break the butter into chunks and toss into the flour to coat. Gently rub the butter into the flour – you need to see chunks of butter. If you are using ready-rolled puff pastry, skip to step 6.

2 Make a well in the centre of the flour and, using a round-bladed knife, add three-quarters of the water and mix well. Keep adding the water bit by bit until you have a firm dough. Cover the bowl with a clean damp tea towel and pop it in the fridge for 20 minutes to rest.

3 Tip the dough onto a lightly floured surface and shape into a rectangle using your hands. Using a rolling pin, roll out the dough to a large rectangle (you will see streaks of butter) then fold the top third down to the centre and the bottom up to cover the top as you would to fold a letter. Use the rolling pin to shape each side so it stays neat.

4 Give the dough a quarter turn and repeat the above process. Wrap in cling film or parchment and chill for 20 minutes.

5 Repeat the process three or four more times in the same way to build up the layers and chill until ready to use.

6 Preheat the oven to 180°C (160°C fan oven) Gas 4.

7 Lightly scrub the carrots, place whole in a baking dish along with the honey and balsamic vinegar and toss well. Roast for 30–40 minutes until the carrots are tender but still have their colour, and leave to cool. One cooled, cut the carrots in half lengthways.

⇶→

8 Preheat the oven to 220°C (200°C fan oven) Gas 7. Roll out the chilled pastry onto a sheet of baking parchment to a rectangle approximately 35 x 25cm/14 x 10in, or simply unroll the ready-rolled sheet onto a baking sheet lined with baking parchment. Score a border around the edge of the pastry approximately 1 inch in, being careful not to cut all the way through.

9 Prick the centre base with a fork and bake for 8–10 minutes until lightly golden, pushing the middle down with the back of a spoon. Turn the oven down to 200°C (180°C fan oven) Gas 6.

10 Blitz the cooked beetroot in a food processor and mix well with the soft cheese in a bowl. Spread the beetroot cream cheese over the base and lay the carrots on top. Scatter with a little chopped rosemary and thyme and bake for 12–15 minutes until golden brown.

My BIG summer pavlova!

YOU WILL NEED A BAKING SHEET

————

I shared this pavlova on my Instagram page and couldn't believe the response. Everyone loved it, it was a huge hit and was shared by so many accounts. Pavlova is a great favourite in my house, and this is a real showstopper! I love topping the crispy mallowy shell with seasonal fruits depending on the time of year I make it.

SERVES 8–10

For the meringue
6 large egg whites
340g/12oz caster sugar
1 tsp cornflour

For the roasted fruits
200g/7oz mixture of rhubarb
    and strawberries
Drizzle of honey, to taste
1 tbsp rum (optional)

For the strawberry coulis
150g/5oz strawberries, washed
    and hulled
30g/1oz icing sugar
Splash of lemon juice

For the chantilly cream
400ml/14fl oz double cream
2 tbsp icing sugar
1 tsp vanilla bean paste

To decorate
Few fresh strawberries
    and blueberries
Edible flowers

Tip
Once topped with cream, the pavlova is best eaten straight away as the cream and fruits soften the meringue shell and it can go a little soft and crack.

1 Start by roasting the fruits. Preheat your oven to 200°C (180°C fan oven) Gas 6.

2 Cut the rhubarb into 2.5cm/1in pieces and leave the strawberries whole, removing the leaves and stalks. Place in a heatproof bowl and add a good drizzle of honey and the rum. Roast the fruits for 10–15 minutes, until softened but still holding their shape, reserving the syrup to drizzle over the pavlova later. Leave to cool completely.

3 Preheat the oven to 150°C (130°C fan oven) Gas 2. Draw a 20cm/8in circle on baking paper using a plate or the base of a cake tin, then flip it over and place on a baking sheet.

4 For the meringue, whisk the egg whites in a stand mixer until they form soft peaks. Add the sugar a spoonful at a time, whisking well in between each addition until all the sugar has dissolved. Test the meringue by rubbing a little of the mixture between your fingers. The meringue should be smooth and you shouldn't feel any grains of sugar. Add the cornflour and briefly mix.

5 Place a little dab of the meringue on each corner of the baking paper so it sticks to the baking sheet. Dollop the meringue inside the drawn circle and make a cavity in the top with the back of a spoon. Then shape the dome by smoothing a palette knife from the base upwards to create a little spike, shaping inwards slightly as you reach the top to create a bulbous shape.

6 Bake for 15 minutes, then reduce the oven to 110°C (90°C fan oven) Gas ¼ and bake for a further 2½–3 hours until dry to the touch. Leave in the oven to cool completely, ideally overnight.

⟫➤

7 For the coulis, place the hulled strawberries in a small saucepan with the icing sugar and lemon juice and simmer for 10–15 minutes until the strawberries have broken down. Blend the strawberries until very smooth and push through a fine sieve. Set to one side.

8 Make the chantilly cream by whisking the double cream with the icing sugar and vanilla in a bowl until light and pillowy.

9 To assemble, place the pavlova shell on a serving plate or cake stand. Dollop the cream into the cavity and top with the cooled roasted fruits. Add the remaining fresh fruits and drizzle over the juices from the reserved syrup from the roasted fruits, and a little coulis if you fancy. Then top with pretty edible flowers and eat straight away.

Vanilla panna cotta with a mango and passionfruit sauce

YOU WILL NEED A SELECTION OF JARS OR PANNA COTTA MOULDS

―――――――

Liven up this classic Italian creamy dessert with my take on the delicately flavoured sweet. The tropical flavours are sure to tickle your tastebuds! The ideal light treat for a summer get-together, barbecue or party.

SERVES 4–5

For the panna cotta
2 sheets of gelatine
400ml/14fl oz double cream
140ml/5fl oz milk
50g/1½oz golden caster sugar
1 tsp vanilla bean paste
½ tsp coconut extract

For the sauce
½ mango, peeled and chopped
50ml/1½fl oz water
4–5 passionfruit
2 tbsp caster sugar

To serve
Passionfruit pips
Desiccated coconut
Diced mango
Edible flowers

1 Soak the gelatine sheets in water for around 5 minutes until soft. (If you want to make your panna cotta in moulds, add an extra sheet of gelatine.)

2 Pour the cream and milk into a small saucepan, add the sugar and heat gently until simmering, then remove from heat. Add the vanilla and coconut extract to the pan. Squeeze the water from the gelatine, add it to the milky mixture and stir well to dissolve thoroughly, then set aside to cool slightly.

3 Pour the panna cotta into moulds, or pop into four or five jars like I have here.

4 Place the jars or moulds into the fridge to set for a few hours or preferably overnight.

5 For the sauce, blitz the mango and water in a food processor. Pour into a saucepan with the pulp from the passionfruit and the sugar, then heat on a medium heat, stirring, until thick. Push through a sieve into a bowl, reserving a few pips for decoration.

6 To serve, remove the jars from the fridge (if using moulds, place a plate on top and flip over to release). Top with spoonfuls of the fruity sauce, scatter over a few passionfruit pips and decorate with a little desiccated coconut, diced mango and edible flowers.

Tip
Keep old jam jars as they often come in handy to serve pretty desserts in.

Flower-power salted caramel brownies

YOU WILL NEED A 23CM/9IN SQUARE TIN OR BROWNIE TIN

My indulgent, rich and fudgy brownies with a layer of salted caramel running through the middle aren't just super tasty, they're also a feast for the eyes. I've topped these brownies with a layer of ganache and pressed in some seasonal edible flowers from our garden to give them a floral touch.

MAKES 16

For the brownies
225g/8oz unsalted butter,
    plus extra for greasing
225g/8oz dark chocolate drops
350g/12½oz jar of caramel
1½ tsp flaky sea salt
4 large eggs
125g/4½oz light muscovado sugar
100g/3½oz caster sugar
140g/5oz plain flour
60g/2oz cocoa powder

For the ganache
200ml/7fl oz double cream
200g/7oz milk chocolate drops

Fresh/dried edible flowers,
    to decorate

1   Preheat the oven to 180°C (160°C fan oven) Gas 4. Lightly grease the tin and line with baking parchment, making sure it overhangs the edges.

2   Melt the butter in a saucepan, add the chocolate drops and stir to melt. Leave to cool a little.

3   Put the caramel in a small bowl and mix to loosen, then add the flaky salt and mix well.

4   Whisk the eggs and sugars in a large bowl, adding 100g/3½oz of the salted caramel, and whisk until thick. Add the cooled chocolate mixture and mix well. Sift the flour and cocoa over the mixture and gently mix.

5   Pour half the batter into the tin, then spoon the remaining caramel on top leaving a 1cm/½in border around the edge. Level with a spatula and top with the remaining brownie mixture.

6   Bake the brownie for 35–40 minutes until risen and a crust has formed on the top with a slight wobble in the centre. Leave to cool completely in the tin on a cooling rack.

7   To make the ganache, heat the cream in a small saucepan until steaming, then add in the chocolate drops and mix until melted. Once the brownie has cooled, pour the ganache all over the top and leave to set.

8   Using the baking parchment, gently lift the brownie out of the tin and press edible flowers onto the top. Using a sharp knife, cut into equal squares or rectangles.

Tip
You can also make ganache by heating the cream and chocolate together in the microwave in 30-second bursts until smooth and silky

Rhubarb, blueberry & strawberry mini cobblers

YOU WILL NEED 4 RAMEKINS OR ONE LARGE DISH

Who could resist a fruity, syrupy pud topped with a golden,
buttery biscuity topping and packed with delicious summery fruits?
I love mine still warm out of the oven with a scoop or two of ice cream!

SERVES 4

For the cobbler topping
70g/2½oz unsalted butter
140g/5oz self-raising flour
50g/1½oz caster sugar
60ml/2fl oz milk
1 egg yolk

For the fruity filling
300g/10½oz rhubarb
300g/10½oz strawberries
130g/4½oz blueberries
50g/1½oz soft brown sugar
Zest and juice of 1 orange
2 tbsp cornflour

1 For the cobbler topping, rub the butter and flour together in a bowl with your fingertips until you have fine breadcrumbs, then add the sugar, milk and egg yolk and mix well. Pop the bowl into the fridge for the mixture to firm up.

2 Preheat the oven to 190°C (170°C fan oven) Gas 5. Chop the rhubarb into small batons and quarter the strawberries. Toss the fruits in the sugar, juice, zest and cornflour and mix well.

3 Fill small ramekins with the fruits, or alternatively you can make one larger cobbler in a dish.

4 Remove the cobbler topping from the fridge and roll into rough balls varying in size.

5 Arrange the balls on top of the fruity mixture, leaving gaps in between as the topping will spread as it bakes.

6 Bake for 30–35 minutes until the topping is golden brown and fruity juices are bubbling around the sides.

Lemon & lime curd meringue cups

YOU WILL NEED A 12-HOLE MINI MUFFIN TIN, A PIPING BAG & A STAR NOZZLE,
& A BLOWTORCH (OPTIONAL)

————

I love a meringue pie but these mini lemon and lime cups are the perfect addition
to an afternoon tea or make the cutest little canapés. Crunchy, buttery
biscuit shells are filled with zingy curd and topped with silky sweet torched
meringue. I use a mini muffin tin for these so they are bitesize.

MAKES 12

For the biscuit base
60g/2oz butter
30g/1oz caster sugar
90g/3oz plain flour
Zest of 1 small lemon

For the Swiss meringue
2 large egg whites
120g/4oz caster sugar
½ tsp cream of tartar
1 tsp vanilla bean paste

Lemon and Lime Curd (p. 186)

1   To make the biscuit base, beat the butter and sugar together in a bowl, then add the flour and zest and bring together by kneading in the bowl. Divide the dough into 12 equal pieces and place a piece in each hole of the tin. Working with one piece at a time, use your fingers to tease the dough up the sides of the tin, pressing it into the corners. Pop the tin into the fridge for half an hour to firm up.

2   Preheat your oven to 200°C (180°C fan oven) Gas 6, then bake the cups for 10–12 minutes until golden. Leave to cool, then gently remove them from the tin and place on a platter or plate.

3   For the Swiss meringue, add the egg whites and sugar to a grease-free heatproof bowl and set over a pan of simmering water. I use the bowl of my stand mixer for this. Gently whisk and heat the mixture until you can't feel any sugar grains when you rub a little between your fingers.

4   Transfer the bowl to the mixer and whisk until the bowl has completely cooled and the meringue is thick and glossy. Finally add the cream of tartar and vanilla and whisk a little more.

5   Spoon the meringue into a piping bag fitted with a star piping nozzle.

6   To assemble, fill the cups with zingy curd and pipe a star of meringue on top.

7   Use a blowtorch or pop the cups under a hot grill to colour the meringue.

Tip
Ensure all equipment for the Swiss meringue is grease-free. I wipe the inside of the bowl and the whisk with a little lemon juice or vinegar and dry with a paper towel. The meringue will not whip up if there is any greasy residue. Same goes for any egg yolk – separate the eggs into a cup first to make sure the yolk doesn't find its way to the bowl!

Asparagus, broad bean & pea tart

YOU WILL NEED A 36 X 12CM/14 X 5IN BAKING TIN

This creamy, cheesy tart in a crisp, buttery pastry case is suitable for vegetarians and is the perfect summer tart to pack for a picnic or eat in the garden with a light side salad for lunch.

SERVES 6–8

For the pastry
200g/7oz plain flour
90g/3oz unsalted butter
2–3 tbsp cold water
35g/1oz mature Cheddar cheese, grated

For the filling
3 medium eggs
200ml/7fl oz double cream
1 tbsp fresh chives, chopped
Salt and pepper
120g/4oz mature Cheddar cheese
50g/1½oz broad beans (podded)
50g/1½oz garden peas
1 large bunch of asparagus, woody stalks remove

1 To make the pastry, rub the flour and butter in a bowl until it resembles breadcrumbs. Add water a little at a time until the dough comes together. Add the grated cheese, mix well and flatten to a flat rectangular shape. Do not overwork the dough or it will be tough. Wrap it in baking parchment and pop into the fridge to rest for half an hour.

2 Roll out the pastry on a lightly floured worktop to approximately 3mm thick. Lift the pastry into the tin, pressing into the corners and allowing the pastry to overhang the edges. Prick the base of the pastry and pop it back into the fridge for 20 minutes to chill.

3 Preheat the oven to 220°C (200°C fan oven) Gas 7. Line the chilled pastry case with baking parchment and fill with baking beans or rice. Bake for 15 minutes, remove the beans and paper carefully and bake for 5 minutes more.

4 Trim the edges of the pastry carefully using a sharp knife or vegetable peeler, and leave to cool.

5 Turn the oven down to 180°C (160°C fan oven) Gas 4. For the filling, crack the eggs into a jug and whisk. Add the cream, herbs, salt and pepper.

6 Grate the Cheddar and scatter over the base of the tart case, reserving a little, then arrange the broad beans, peas and asparagus on top.

7 Pour the creamy mixture on top of the vegetables and scatter with the reserved grated cheese.

8 Bake for 30–35 minutes until the tart is golden and still has a slight wobble in the centre. Leave to cool in the tin on a cooling rack.

Tip
When making pastry, try not to overwork the dough as it will become tough and be more likely to shrink during cooking.

Blueberry & white chocolate cheesecake

YOU WILL NEED A 20CM/8IN ROUND LOOSE-BOTTOMED TIN, A FOOD PROCESSOR & A PIPING BAG

————

With the sheer abundance of blueberries in our garden in the summer, it's difficult not to pick and eat them all straight from the bushes! This no-bake light and creamy cheesecake on a buttery biscuit base is so delicious and a real crowd pleaser!

SERVES 12

For the cheesecake
20 digestive biscuits
150g/5oz unsalted butter, melted
300g/10½oz white chocolate drops
500g/1 lb 1½oz full fat cream cheese
80g/3oz icing sugar
1 tsp vanilla bean paste
300ml/11fl oz double cream
150g/5oz fresh blueberries
2 tbsp freeze-dried blueberry pieces

For the meringue kisses
1 large egg white
60g/2oz caster sugar
¼ tsp cream of tartar
¼ tsp vanilla bean paste

To decorate
Blueberries
Edible flowers

Tip
Use a little of the mixture to stick the parchment to the baking sheet in all four corners.

It's best to make this cheesecake a day in advance as it sets firmly overnight in the fridge and is easier to slice when it's firm and holds its shape.

1 Blitz the biscuits in a food processor to fine crumbs and add the melted butter, then mix well. Press the biscuit mixture into the base of the tin using the back of a spoon.

2 Melt the white chocolate drops in the microwave in 30-second bursts until melted. Leave to cool.

3 Whisk the cream cheese, icing sugar and vanilla together until smooth. Add the double cream and melted chocolate and whisk until thick, then divide the mixture equally between two bowls.

4 Pour one bowl of the creamy cheesecake mix onto the biscuit base and smooth with a palette knife.

5 Lightly whizz the fresh blueberries in a food processor and fold through the second bowl of creamy mixture. Add the freeze-dried blueberries to the mix and gently pour on top of the white mix, smoothing gently. Place the cheesecake in the fridge for a few hours to set, preferably overnight.

6 For the meringue kisses, preheat the oven to 120°C (100°C fan oven) Gas ½ and line a baking sheet with baking parchment.

7 Place the egg white and sugar in a grease-free heatproof bowl over a pan of simmering water, making sure the bowl doesn't touch the water. (I use the bowl of my stand mixer for this.) Whisk the mixture over the pan on a medium heat until you can't feel any sugar grains when you rub a little mixture between your fingers.

8 Once ready, take off the heat and whisk until cooled, thick and glossy. Add the cream of tartar and vanilla then whisk a little more. Transfer the meringue to a piping bag with a nozzle of your choice – I use a small star and round nozzle for mine. Pipe small shapes onto the baking paper and bake for 30–35 minutes until they are dry to touch and lift off the paper easily.

9 To assemble, carefully remove the cheesecake from the tin and place onto a cake stand or plate. Decorate by adding the meringue kisses and blueberries around the edge and add a few edible petals for a pop of colour.

Raspberry & rose Bakewell tart

YOU WILL NEED A 20CM/8IN ROUND TART TIN

This Bakewell tart is divine! The crisp buttery pastry shell holds a
thick layer of raspberry and rose jam, soft frangipane filling and
a sweet icing topped with fresh raspberries.

SERVES 8

For the pastry
100g/3½oz unsalted butter, chilled
200g/7oz plain flour, plus extra
    for dusting
40g/1½oz icing sugar
1 medium egg, beaten
2 tbsp cold water

Raspberry and Rose Jam
    (see p.184)

For the filling
180g/6½oz unsalted butter
180g/6½oz caster sugar
3 medium eggs, beaten
180g/6½oz ground almonds
1 tsp almond extract

For the icing
150g/5oz icing sugar
½ –¾ tsp water
Pink food gel

To decorate
Fresh raspberries
Dried rose buds

Tip
I often use a vegetable peeler to trim
off the excess pastry once blind
baked as it's a little more gentle
than a knife. The frangipane filling
can be a little thick to spread, so I
often use a piping bag to pipe the
mixture in so it doesn't disturb the
jam too much.

1   For the pastry, dice the cold butter and add to a bowl along
with the flour. Rub the mixture together with your fingers until it
resembles fine breadcrumbs. Add the icing sugar and gently mix.

2   Add the beaten egg and work the mixture together until it
comes together into a ball. Add a little water if the mixture is dry,
but it shouldn't be sticky so you may not need any.

3   Lightly dust your worktop with a little flour, roll the pastry out
slightly larger than the tin, then carefully lift the pastry into the
tin using the rolling pin to help you. Push the pastry into the
corners with your fingers, leaving a little overhanging the sides.
Place the tin into the fridge to rest for half an hour.

4   Preheat your oven to 190°C (170°C fan oven) Gas 5.

5   Remove the tin from the fridge and line it with baking
parchment. Fill the case with baking beans and bake for
15 minutes. Remove the beans and parchment carefully and
bake for a further 10–15 minutes until the pastry is dry to touch.
Carefully trim the overhanging pastry and leave to cool.

6   Preheat the oven to 180°C (160°C fan oven) Gas 4. For the
filling, beat the butter and sugar together in a large bowl, then
add the beaten eggs and ground almonds. Add the almond
extract and mix well.

7   Mix the jam with a spoon to loosen a little, add 5–6 tbsp to
the pastry case and spread smooth with a palette knife. Top with
the almond filling, smooth with a palette knife and bake for
35–40 minutes until set, then leave to cool.

8   Once the tart is completely cool, make the icing by adding a
little water to the icing sugar until you have a thick glossy icing.

9   To assemble, pile raspberries in the centre of the tart and
gently spoon the white icing all around them to flood the top,
reserving a little.

10 Add a drop of pink food gel to the remaining icing and mix
well. Add a few blobs of the icing here and there, then drag a
skewer through the pink icing to create a little swirl. Leave the
icing to set and decorate with dried rose buds.

Hazelnut & caramel floral cake

YOU WILL NEED 3 X 15CM/6IN ROUND CAKE TINS, A PIPING BAG & ROUND NOZZLE

This cake has a wonderful hazelnut flavour through it, so if you're a hazelnut fan, it won't disappoint. To make this cake the star of the show, decorate with edible flowers all over – it will make you smile and brighten up anyone's day!

SERVES 8-10

For the cake
165g/6oz unsalted butter, plus extra for greasing
250g/9oz golden caster sugar
1½ tsp vanilla bean paste
65ml/2fl oz vegetable oil
50g/1½oz hazelnut paste
4 large eggs
250g/9oz plain flour
1 tsp baking powder
2½ tbsp milk, to loosen

For the filling
6 tbsp caramel

For the hazelnut Swiss meringue buttercream
4 large egg whites
300g/10½oz caster sugar
400g/14oz unsalted butter
150g/5oz hazelnut paste
1 tsp vanilla bean paste

Fresh seasonal flowers and petals, to decorate

Tip
When whipping up the meringue, make sure the bowl is completely cold to touch before adding the butter. From time to time, Swiss meringue can be temperamental! If it looks curdled, keep whipping and it will come back together. If it looks soupy, pop the whole bowl into the fridge for approximately 20 minutes and whip again.

1 Preheat the oven to 180°C (160°C fan oven) Gas 4 and lightly grease and line the base of each tin.

2 In a bowl or a stand mixer, beat the butter and sugar until light and fluffy.

3 Add the vanilla, oil and hazelnut paste and mix well.

4 Whisk the eggs and add half into the mixture along with half the flour and baking powder. Mix well and add the remaining eggs and flour to the mixture. Add enough milk to loosen the cake batter and divide equally between the tins. Bake for 30–35 minutes until risen or until a skewer comes out clean when poked in the middle.

5 Leave the cakes to cool in the tins for 10 minutes, then turn out and leave to cool completely on a cooling rack.

6 For the Swiss meringue, add the egg whites and sugar to a grease-free heatproof bowl and set over a pan of simmering water. I use the bowl of my stand mixer for this. Gently whisk and heat the mixture until you can't feel any sugar grains when you rub a little between your fingers. Transfer the bowl to the mixer and whisk until the bowl has completely cooled and the meringue is thick and glossy. Switch to a paddle beater.

7 Chop the butter into cubes and add a cube at a time, mixing well between each addition. Once all the butter has been added, add the hazelnut paste and vanilla and mix until thick and smooth. Spoon half of the mixture into a piping bag fitted with a large round nozzle.

8 To assemble, level the tops of the cakes if they have peaked slightly.

9 Place one layer of sponge onto a cake stand, securing it with a blob of buttercream. Spread a little buttercream on top, then pipe a circle of buttercream around the edge, 1cm/½in in from the side. Spoon 2 tbsp caramel into the middle and smooth with a palette knife. Continue with the next sponge in the same way, then top with the remaining sponge. Pipe rings of buttercream all up the sides and over the top of the cake, smoothing with a cake scraper and levelling the top. Place the cake into the fridge to firm up for half an hour.

10 To decorate, press a selection of edible flowers all over the sides and top of the cake, overlapping a few so you can't see the buttercream underneath.

Mini summer blueberry galettes

YOU WILL NEED BAKING SHEETS

Seeing as it's blueberry season, I couldn't resist making these mini
sweet and tart fruity galettes in flaky pastry. They are the perfect,
rustic fuss-free pud and even better topped with a scoop of ice cream!

SERVES 6

For the pastry
160g/5½oz plain flour
50g/1½oz icing sugar
80g/3oz unsalted butter
1 egg yolk

Or 1 sheet of ready-rolled sweet
   shortcrust pastry

For the filling
50g/1½oz Strawberry & vanilla jam
   (see p.184)
1½ tsp cornflour
200g/7oz blueberries

1 small egg/splash of milk
1 tbsp demerara sugar

1   For the pastry, sift the flour and icing sugar into a large bowl
and cut the butter into cubes. Toss the butter into the flour and
coat well.

2   Rub the butter into the flour until it resembles breadcrumbs,
then add the egg yolk and gently work the dough until it comes
together. If the pastry is a little dry add a splash of water.

3   Turn the dough onto the worktop, shape it into a disc shape
and wrap in baking parchment, then chill for 30 minutes in the
fridge.

4   Meanwhile, put the jam into a small bowl and mix to loosen.
Add the cornflour and mix well. Add the blueberries to the bowl
and stir gently.

5   Roll out the chilled pastry to the thickness of a pound coin and
cut out circles approximately 10cm/4in wide. Carefully lift the
discs and place onto baking trays lined with baking parchment.
Keep rolling and cutting until you've used up all the pastry. Pile
the fruit up in the centre of the pastry discs, then fold up the
edges to create pleats, overlapping as you go.

6   Pop the galettes into the fridge for 20 minutes to firm up, and
preheat your oven to 200°C (180°C fan oven) Gas 6.

7   Beat the egg, then lightly egg wash the galettes and sprinkle
with demerara sugar. Bake for 20–25 minutes until golden and the
fruits are bubbling.

Tip
Do not overwork the dough or it
will become tough and chewy.

Salsa verde courgette pizza

YOU WILL NEED A BAKING SHEET, PIZZA TRAY OR BAKE STONE

————

We spend a lot of time in the garden during the summer and love getting the pizza oven out. Nothing beats picking the fresh herbs and veggies right from the garden to put straight on our pizzas. Courgettes are easy to grow, versatile, healthy, tender and great to cook with. This is my go-to recipe on pizza night – the garlicky buttered base with fragrant, vibrant and fresh salsa verde, courgette ribbons and crunchy pine nuts is the best combination ever!

SERVES 3

For the pizza dough
300g/10½oz strong white
  bread flour
1 tsp fine salt
1 tsp fast-action yeast
1 tbsp olive oil, plus extra
  for greasing
160ml/5½fl oz warm water

For the garlic butter
150g/5oz unsalted butter
2 garlic cloves, crushed
1 tsp chopped parsley
½ tsp flaky salt

For the salsa verde
1 small shallot
2 garlic cloves
3 anchovy fillets
2 tsp capers
2 tbsp fresh parsley
2 tbsp fresh basil
½ tbsp fresh chives
2 tbsp fresh mint
4 small gherkins
1 tsp Dijon mustard
1 tbsp red wine vinegar
4–6 tbsp olive oil
Pepper, to taste

For the toppings
2 small courgettes
Pine nuts
½ mozzarella ball, torn
Rocket

1 To make the dough, tip the flour into a bowl, add the salt to one side and the yeast to the other. Add the oil and water, then mix together with your hands until the dough comes together in a ball. Tip the dough onto the worktop and stretch and knead for about 10 minutes until the dough becomes smooth and elastic.

2 Lightly oil a bowl, pop the dough in, cover with a clean damp tea towel and leave to prove until doubled in size.

3 Meanwhile, make the garlic butter. Beat the butter until smooth, then add the crushed garlic, chopped parsley and flaky salt and mix well. Leave out at room temperature.

4 For the salsa verde, finely chop all the dry ingredients, add the mustard, vinegar and oil and mix well. Season with pepper to taste.

5 Use a vegetable peeler to take long ribbons off the courgette and lay them on a clean tea towel to absorb the moisture.

6 Preheat the oven to 220°C (200°C fan oven) Gas 7, or as hot as it will go, and place a baking sheet, bake stone or pizza tray inside to heat up. Alternatively, cook in an outdoor pizza oven. Once the dough has doubled in size, divide it into three pieces. Roll each piece into a ball, then, using a rolling pin or your hands, shape each piece into a large thin rough circle.

7 Carefully remove the baking sheet or tray from the oven and place the pizza base on top. Spread over the garlic butter and pile courgette ribbons on top. Spoon over the salsa verde and scatter over the pine nuts. Push torn pieces of mozzarella in between the toppings and bake for 8–10 minutes until golden, blistered and bubbling.

8 Top your pizza with extra salsa verde if you fancy, and pile on some fresh rocket.

Rhubarb & custard puff pockets

YOU WILL NEED CUTTERS (OPTIONAL) & A BAKING SHEET

If you're like me and spent your pocket money buying rhubarb and custard sweets as a child, these puff pockets with the classic flavour will not disappoint!

SERVES 4

Rough puff pastry (p.62) or 1 sheet of ready-rolled puff pastry

2 long sticks of rhubarb (approx. 220g/7½oz)
50g/1½oz caster sugar
½ tsp vanilla bean paste

For the custard
150ml/5½fl oz whole milk
½ tsp vanilla bean paste
1 egg yolk
1 tbsp caster sugar
1¼ tsp cornflour

1 egg
½ tbsp granulated sugar, to sprinkle
Icing sugar, to dust

1 Chop the rhubarb into small batons and place in a saucepan along with the sugar and vanilla. Heat on a medium heat for about 5 minutes until rhubarb is soft but still holding its shape. Leave to cool.

2 For the custard, pour the milk and vanilla into a small saucepan and bring to the boil. Leave to cool slightly.

3 In a medium-sized bowl, whisk the egg yolk, sugar and cornflour together, then add the milk and whisk well. Pour the mixture back into the saucepan and heat on medium until very thick, making sure the mixture doesn't catch and burn on the bottom of the pan.

4 Pour the custard into a bowl, covering the surface with cling film to stop a skin forming.

5 Roll out the pastry to a large rectangle of about 3mm thickness or unroll the ready-rolled pastry. Cut into eight equal rectangles, and stamp out shapes in four of them (I use a heart-shaped cutter for mine), or feel free to leave them plain.

6 Line a baking sheet with baking parchment and lift the four plain bases carefully onto it. Spread a quarter of the custard in the centre of a pastry, leaving a border around the edge, then top the custard with a quarter of the rhubarb. Beat the egg and lightly egg wash the border, then lift the top piece on top. Seal the edges with a fork or crimp using your thumb and fingers. Continue with the remaining pastries, then brush the tops with a little more beaten egg and sprinkle with sugar.

7 Bake for 15–20 minutes until puffed up and golden brown and dust with a little icing sugar.

Tomato, raspberry & mozzarella galette

YOU WILL NEED A BAKING SHEET

This colourful galette is a real taste of summer, taking the everyday and making it into something truly amazing. The pastry melts in the mouth and the filling is zingy, fresh and deliciously sweet. Tomatoes and raspberries are an unusual but great flavour combination – it really does work!

SERVES 4

For the pastry
150g/5oz plain flour
½ tsp sea salt
¼ tsp cracked black pepper
15g/½oz mature Cheddar cheese, finely grated
110g/4oz unsalted butter, cold
100ml/3½fl oz ice-cold water

For the filling
450g/1 lb tomatoes
15–20 fresh raspberries
½ mozzarella ball
½ tbsp fresh mint
½ tbsp fresh basil

1 egg, beaten
½ tsp coarse sea salt

Fresh basil, to garnish

Tip
When making this galette, I often reserve the tomato seeds and dry them out on a paper towel. These can then be planted in seed trays then into plant pots to grow tomatoes the following spring!

1 For the pastry, tip the flour, salt, pepper and cheese in a bowl, then coarsely grate in the cold butter and mix all the ingredients together with your fingertips to create breadcrumbs.

2 Add the ice-cold water and use a round-bladed knife to bring the dough together into a ball. Flatten the dough into a disc shape, wrap in baking parchment and chill for 30 minutes.

3 Preheat your oven to 220°C (200°C fan oven) Gas 7. Slice the tomatoes and scoop out the majority of the seeds, then lay the tomatoes on a paper towel to absorb the liquid. (You don't have to do this, but while baking, the juices run and make the pastry soggy.)

4 Remove the pastry from the fridge and roll out onto a lightly floured sheet of baking parchment, making a rough circle approximately 35cm/14in wide. Arrange the tomatoes and raspberries on top of the pastry, leaving a 5cm/2in border all around the edge.

5 Fold up the sides of the dough, overlapping the pieces and pressing to seal.

6 Tear the mozzarella and place on top and in between the fruits, then scatter the herbs on top.

7 Brush the edges with beaten egg and scatter a few pinches of salt over the edges of the pastry. Carefully slide the parchment onto a baking tray and bake for 10 minutes.

8 Reduce the temperature to 190°C (170°C fan oven) Gas 5 and bake for a further 20–25 minutes until golden brown and bubbling. Top with fresh basil to serve.

Mini pistachio, raspberry & rose cakes

YOU WILL NEED A 12-HOLE LOOSE-BOTTOMED MUFFIN TIN, A PIPING BAG & ROUND NOZZLE

Delicious layers of pistachio-studded cake, with a sweet delicate floral twist!
These little cakes are super cute and would be great for any
sort of get-together with friends and family.

MAKES 12

For the mini cakes
170g/6oz unsalted butter
170g/6oz golden caster sugar
3 large eggs, beaten
¼ tsp pistachio flavouring
170g/6oz plain flour
1 tsp baking powder
50g/1½oz pistachios, finely chopped

For the filling
200ml/7fl oz double cream
½ tsp vanilla bean paste
¼ tsp rose water

Raspberry and Rose Jam
   (see p.184)

For the icing
140g/5oz icing sugar
½ tsp rose water
Pink food gel
3–4 tsp water

To decorate
Fresh raspberries
Freeze-dried raspberries

1 Preheat the oven to 200°C (180°C fan oven) Gas 6 and lightly grease the holes of the tin.

2 Beat the butter and sugar together until light and pale, then gradually add the beaten eggs and pistachio flavouring.

3 Sift the flour and baking powder on top and fold through along with the finely chopped pistachios.

4 Divide the mixture between the holes of the tin and level with the back of a spoon.

5 Bake for 15–20 minutes or until a skewer comes out clean when poked in the centre.

6 Leave to cool slightly, then remove each cake carefully and place onto a cooling rack to cool completely. Once cold, trim any peaks off the tops and slice each cake in half.

7 Loosen the jam slightly with a spoon, then add a dollop of jam to the base half of each cake.

8 For the filling, whisk the double cream, vanilla and rose water together until pillowy and place into a piping bag fitted with a round nozzle.

9 Pipe small cream peaks on top of the jam on each sponge, with a larger peak in the centre, then top with the top half of each cake.

10 To make the icing, add rose water to the icing sugar and a little pink food gel. Add the water a little at a time; you may not need it all. The icing should be thick enough to drizzle but not so thin that it runs off the cakes.

11 Working on one cake at a time, spoon over some of the icing, encouraging it to drip down the sides a little. Decorate the top with fresh raspberries and freeze-dried raspberry pieces.

Zaatar tortilla wraps with sweetcorn salsa & yoghurt dip

YOU WILL NEED A HEAVY-BASED FRYING PAN

Forget shop-bought tortillas, give these a try! The sweetcorn salsa is super easy to prepare and even tastier topped with the yoghurt dip. The fresh taste of summer in a wrap.

MAKES 8 LARGE OR
16 SMALL WRAPS

For the wraps
300g/10½oz plain flour
½ tsp fine salt
½ tsp baking powder
1 tbsp ground zaatar
125ml/4½fl oz warm water
35ml/1fl oz vegetable oil

For the sweetcorn salsa
Splash of oil, for frying
2 sweetcorn cobs
1 red onion, finely chopped
1 avocado, peeled, stoned and diced
1 red pepper, deseeded and finely chopped
1 red chilli, deseeded and finely chopped
1 tbsp coriander, finely chopped
Zest and juice of 1 lime
100g/3½oz feta cheese, crumbled

For the yoghurt dip
200g/7oz natural yoghurt
1 garlic clove, crushed
1 tbsp olive oil
Juice of ½ lemon
1½ tsp ground sumac
Salt and pepper, to taste

Tips
Wrapping the tortillas in a clean tea towel or foil while cooking the rest will keep the wraps soft.

You can add cooked meats or extra veggies to the wraps too.

1   For the salsa, place the corn cobs in a medium-hot frying pan with a little oil. Cook the corn, turning regularly, for 8–10 minutes until evenly toasted. Remove from the pan, and when cool enough to handle, slice the corn from the cobs using a sharp knife and place in a bowl.

2   Finely chop the onion, avocado, pepper, chilli and coriander and add to the bowl. Toss together, then add the lime juice and zest and crumble over the feta cheese. Mix well and set to one side for later.

3   For the dip, mix the yoghurt, crushed garlic, oil, lemon juice and sumac together in a bowl, then season with salt and pepper to taste. Pop in the fridge for the flavours to infuse.

4   To make the wraps, mix the flour, salt, baking powder and zaatar in a bowl, then add the water and oil. Mix well until the dough comes together, then knead on the worktop until smooth and elastic.

5   Weigh the dough and divide it into equal pieces. Depending on size, this recipe makes 16 small wraps or 8 large. Cover the pieces with a clean tea towel and leave to rest for 10–20 minutes.

6   Roll each piece of dough with a rolling pin. (I use an 11cm/4½in cutter so mine are all even in size, but you don't have to do this. Then I re-roll the scraps until I have used up all the dough.)

7   Heat a heavy-based pan over a medium heat and cook each tortilla for 1½ minutes on one side until starting to blister in places, then flip it over and cook the other side in the same way.

8   Wrap the cooked tortillas in a clean tea towel or a piece of foil while you cook the others.

9   To serve, generously fill the wraps with the sweetcorn salsa and top with the yoghurt dip.

Rhubarb & almond cinnamon buns

YOU WILL NEED A 23 X 30CM/9 X 12IN BAKING TIN & A FOOD PROCESSOR

———————

These soft and fluffy rolls are an absolute seasonal delight
and a take on the classic cinnamon bun with added tart rhubarb,
tangy cream cheese icing and crunchy flaked almonds.

MAKES 12

For the dough

320ml/11fl oz whole milk
50g/1½oz softened butter
500g/1 lb 1½oz strong white
    bread flour
10g fast-action yeast
½ tsp fine salt
35g/1oz soft brown sugar
Olive oil, for greasing

For the filling

100g/3½oz unsalted butter
100g/3½oz soft brown sugar
2 tbsp ground cinnamon
180g/6½oz rhubarb
1 tbsp maple syrup
30g/1oz flaked almonds

For the topping

50g/1½oz rhubarb
50g/1½oz cream cheese
50g/1½oz icing sugar

1 For the dough, pour the milk into a saucepan and add the butter. Heat on low until the butter has melted and leave to cool slightly.

2 In a large bowl, or in the bowl of a stand mixer fitted with a dough hook, add the flour, then the yeast to one side and salt to the other. Add the sugar and the warm milk mixture and mix well. Knead until smooth, elastic and stretchy.

3 Lightly oil a bowl with a little olive oil and place the dough into the bowl to prove. Cover with a clean damp tea towel and leave to double in size.

4 For the filling, soften the butter in a bowl, add the sugar and cinnamon and mix until smooth, then set aside for later. Preheat the oven to 200°C (180°C fan oven) Gas 6. Dice the rhubarb and place in a roasting tin with the maple syrup, then roast for 10–15 minutes until soft but still holding its shape. Leave to cool.

5 Line the tin with baking parchment. Once the dough has risen, tip it onto a lightly floured surface and roll out to a large rectangle measuring 40 x 50cm/16 x 20in. Spread over the buttery sugar mixture with a palette knife, leaving a 1cm/½in gap all around the edge. Top with roasted rhubarb pieces and scatter over the flaked almonds.

6 Starting with the longest end, roll up the dough tightly and, with the seam facing downwards, trim off the ends to neaten. Cut the roll into twelve equal slices and place the buns cut side up, with the ends turning inwards into the tin, leaving a gap between each one so they have room to prove.

7 Cover with a clean damp tea towel and leave to prove until the buns meet and are light and fluffy.

8 Preheat the oven to 200°C (180°C fan oven) Gas 6 and once the buns have risen, bake for 20–25 minutes until lightly golden brown. (If the buns are browning too quickly, cover with foil.)

9 For the icing topping, blitz the rhubarb in a food processor and push through a sieve to remove the juice. Mix the cream cheese to loosen and add the icing sugar. Add the rhubarb juice a little at a time then thoroughly mix until smooth.

10 Remove the baked buns from the oven and leave to cool slightly. Smother or drizzle the rhubarb topping over the buns, pull apart and enjoy!

Strawberry, lavender & black pepper Arctic roll

YOU WILL NEED A 22 X 33CM/9 X 13IN SWISS ROLL TIN

————

I have fond memories of eating Arctic roll as a child after cooked roast Sunday dinner, so I love making this for my family too. For this recipe, I picked lavender from our garden, added the flowers to a jar of caster sugar and left it to infuse for a couple of weeks. The black pepper is an unusual addition to this recipe; it balances the sweetness of this dessert and allows all the subtle fruity flavours to come out.

SERVES 6–8

For the sponge
4 large eggs
120g/4oz lavender-infused
   caster sugar
120g/4oz self-raising flour
Butter, for greasing

For the ice cream
397g/14oz tin of condensed milk
500g/1 lb 1½oz double cream
1 tsp vanilla bean paste
¾–1 tsp cracked black pepper
150g/5oz strawberries
2 tbsp freeze-dried strawberries

To decorate
100g/3½oz Strawberry & vanilla jam
   (see p.184)
Icing sugar
Strawberries
Edible flowers

Tip
The ice cream can be made in advance and left in the freezer until ready to use. Don't panic if your ice cream is a little large for the sponge – pop it to one side to thaw slightly and scrape off any excess.

1   For the ice cream, whisk the condensed milk, cream and vanilla together until it forms soft peaks then add the pepper. Blitz the fresh strawberries in a food processor, fold into the ice cream mixture and whisk until thick. Fold through the freeze-dried strawberries.

2   Roll out two pieces of cling film onto the worktop then dollop ice cream mixture in a line a little longer than the width of the tin down the centre.

3   Fold cling film around the ice cream, and wind the ends to look like a Christmas cracker. Roll back and forth on the worktop for the wrap to tighten and place in the freezer overnight to set.

4   Preheat the oven to 200°C (180°C fan oven) Gas 6, grease a Swiss roll tin and line it with baking parchment. Remove the ice cream from the freezer and place to one side to thaw a little.

5   For the sponge, whisk the eggs and sugar until the mixture is thick and light and leaves a ribbon trail when the whisk is lifted. Sift the flour into the mixture and gently fold together to keep the air in.

6   Pour the mixture gently into the tin and level by tilting the tin from side to side, making sure it reaches the corners. Bake for 10–15 minutes or until a skewer comes out clean. Leave to cool slightly, then turn out onto a large piece of greaseproof paper and spread a little jam over the sponge.

7   Unwrap the ice cream and place on the shortest end of the sponge. Use the paper to help tease the sponge around the ice cream. With the seam facing downwards, wrap in the paper and some cling film and pop in the freezer for a couple of hours to harden.

8   When you are ready to serve, place the Arctic roll on a serving board and sift a little icing sugar all over. Heat the remaining jam a little to loosen then add it to the top of the sponge, encouraging it to drip down the sides in places. Add strawberries to the top and a few edible flowers. Slice and enjoy!

Now we are into autumn, daylight becomes noticeably shorter, but soil temperatures are still warm enough to plant out some veggies. There is still a lot to harvest from summer's growth too. We have a greenhouse so it extends the growing season a little and shelters the tender seedlings from the cold winds we often get in Pembrokeshire. Don't worry if you haven't got one, but you may want to get some fleece to cover and protect your plants.

What to plant

Winter lettuces, rocket, mustard leaves, pak choi, mizuna, Swiss chard and kale are all delicious greens and hardy autumnal plants to grow. Now is the perfect time to plant garlic as it needs a period of cold weather for the single cloves you plant to split and form a new bulb. I like growing elephant garlic for its milder taste; it is delicious roasted with your homegrown potatoes.

What to harvest

Early autumn is when much of what you've planted throughout spring and summer comes together to give you a real glut of fresh fruit and veg to harvest, such as beetroots, peas, beans, mangetout, potatoes, kale, Swiss chard, summer carrots, corn, lettuces and tomatoes.

A mid-season autumnal treat is apples and pears. You can tell pears are ready by lifting up the fruit – if it comes away easily, it's ready. Same for the apples, but give them a good twist and they'll come away. Unblemished, unbruised fruits can be stored for months in a cool dark place.

We love growing pumpkins of different sizes and colours in our garden. The more unusual looking the more intriguing I find them! Aside from carving them out for a Halloween celebration, the versatile pumpkin can be used in soups, roasted or – my favourite – in cake. I have a few delicious recipes using pumpkin in my book – give them a try!

Freezing fruit can be such a good way to preserve flavour and gives you the ability to use homegrown fruit out of season throughout the year.

I often take time in autumn to make lots of jams, curds, chutneys and pickles, which I give as gifts to friends and family over the festive period. Nothing beats a homemade gift.

Tip

Make the most of a free, foraged seasonal treat: the juicy, plump blackberry. You can find them almost anywhere – in hedgerows, along lanes, in woods and fields. You can even pick the leaves to make a bramble tea!

Beetroot & chocolate cake

YOU WILL NEED A 20CM/8IN ROUND CAKE TIN

Beetroot is very sweet and keeps this rich chocolate cake wonderfully moist. The silky smooth ganache topping makes it even more delicious.

SERVES 10

For the cake
250g/9oz beetroot, cooked
   and peeled
170ml/6fl oz buttermilk
1 tsp vanilla bean paste
2 tbsp white wine vinegar
255g/9oz plain flour
2 tsp baking powder
1 tbsp beetroot powder
   (optional)
50g/1½oz cocoa powder
170g/6oz unsalted butter,
   plus extra for greasing
240g/8½oz caster sugar
3 large eggs, beaten
30g/1oz dark chocolate drops

For the ganache
150g/5oz dark chocolate drops
150ml/5½fl oz double cream

1 Preheat the oven to 180°C (160°C fan oven) Gas 4 and lightly grease and line the cake tin.

2 Roughly grate the cooked beetroot into a bowl. Add the buttermilk, vanilla and vinegar and mix.

3 Sift the flour, baking powder, beetroot powder and cocoa powder into a separate bowl.

4 In a large bowl or in your mixer, beat the butter and sugar until light and fluffy. Stir in half the beaten eggs, half the flour mixture and half the beetroot mix. Repeat in the same way, adding the remaining ingredients and gently mixing. Stir through the chocolate drops.

5 Pour the batter into the tin and bake for 55 minutes–1 hour or until a skewer comes out clean.

6 Leave the cake in the tin to cool on a cooling rack for 10–15 minutes, then turn out and leave to cool completely.

7 For the chocolate ganache, put the chocolate drops in a bowl, and heat the cream in a small saucepan over a low heat until just starting to steam. Pour the warm cream over the chocolate and leave for a few minutes to melt, then keep stirring until all the chocolate has melted and the ganache is smooth and silky.

8 Flip the cake over onto a cake stand so the flat bottom is facing up, and pour ganache over the cake just before serving.

Tip
If you're using beetroot from the garden like me, thoroughly wash it, remove the leaves and wrap in foil and cook until tender in the oven. When cool enough to handle, peel. Don't throw away the leaves or stems; you can use them in a salad or gently steam or sauté them.

Plum, apple & cinnamon crumble

YOU WILL NEED A HEATPROOF BOWL OR DISH

———

Crumble is a simple, hearty, comforting fruit recipe topped with
a crisp, nutty, buttery crumb topping that turns the everyday fruit into
a stunning dessert. It's one of my family's favourite puds any time of the year.
Best served with ice cream, custard or cream.

SERVES 4

For the fruity filling
3 Bramley apples
5 large plums
60g/2oz soft brown sugar, or less
    depending on the sweetness
    of the fruits
1½ tsp ground cinnamon

For the crumble top
150g/5oz unsalted butter
320g/11½oz plain flour
55g/2oz soft brown sugar
80g/3oz porridge oats
35g/1oz roasted chopped hazelnuts

1   Preheat your oven to 190°C (170°C fan oven) Gas 5.

2   Peel, core and roughly chop the apples and stone and quarter
the plums. Place all the fruits in a large heatproof bowl or dish
and scatter over the sugar and cinnamon, then roughly toss all
together.

3   To make the crumble topping, rub the butter and flour
together to resemble breadcrumbs, then add the sugar, porridge
oats and nuts and mix thoroughly.

4   Pile the crumble mixture on top of the fruits and bake for
40–45 minutes until the topping is golden brown and the fruit
juices are bubbling around the edges.

Tip
Crumble can be made with any
fruit combination – fresh, frozen
or tinned!

Raspberry, white chocolate & almond loaf cake

YOU WILL NEED A 900G/2 LB LOAF TIN, A FOOD PROCESSOR (OPTIONAL) & PIPING BAG

I make this loaf cake in a food processor and it's so simple and quick to do, perfect for those last-minute visitors or events where you need to take something delicious… and not much washing up! The sweetness of the white chocolate with the sharp raspberries is heavenly and the cake is super light too.

SERVES 8–10

For the cake

150g/5½oz margarine/butter, plus extra for greasing
150g/5½oz caster sugar
150g/5½oz plain flour
1 tsp baking powder
150g/5½oz ground almonds
2 large eggs
2 tsp almond extract
1½ tbsp milk
60g/2oz white chocolate drops
250g/9oz fresh raspberries
Few flaked almonds

To decorate

50g/1½oz icing sugar
Pink food gel
Dried edible cornflower petals
Freeze-dried raspberries

1 Preheat the oven to 180°C (160°C fan oven) Gas 4 and grease and line the loaf tin.

2 Tip the butter, sugar, flour, baking powder, ground almonds, eggs and almond extract into a food processor and blitz until smooth. Add enough milk to loosen then stir through the chocolate drops. You can also do this in a large bowl: add all the ingredients and mix well.

3 Pour half the mixture into the tin, then top with lines of raspberries, reserving a few for the top.

4 Add the rest of the cake mix and top with the remaining raspberries. Scatter a few flaked almonds over the top and bake for 40–50 minutes or until a skewer comes out clean.

5 Leave the cake to cool in the tin on a cooling rack for 10–15 minutes, then turn out and leave to cool completely.

6 To make the icing, place the icing sugar into a small bowl and mix with enough water to make a thick paste. Add a little pink food gel to give the icing a blush pink colour. You can either spoon the icing into a small piping bag and snip off the end, or drizzle it with a teaspoon.

7 To decorate, place the cooled cake onto a board or cake stand, drizzle with icing in a stripe effect along the cake and while the icing is still wet, decorate with freeze-dried raspberries and dried cornflower petals.

Pumpkin Swiss roll
with maple cream filling

YOU WILL NEED A 22 X 33CM/9 X 15IN SWISS ROLL TIN

This deliciously indulgent pumpkin roll recipe is made with pumpkin purée
and filled with a light, pillowy maple whipped cream.

SERVES 6

For the Swiss roll
3 large eggs
200g/7oz caster sugar
150g/5oz pumpkin purée
1 tsp vanilla bean paste
100g/3½oz plain flour
½ tsp baking powder
Pinch of fine salt
1 tsp ground cinnamon
½ tsp ground ginger
Butter, for greasing

For the maple cream
250ml/9fl oz double cream
3–4 tbsp maple syrup
1 tsp vanilla bean paste

Icing sugar, to dust

1 Preheat oven to 200°C (180°C fan oven) Gas 6 and lightly
grease and line the tin with baking parchment.

2 Whisk the eggs and sugar together until smooth and thick,
then add the pumpkin purée and vanilla and whisk again.

3 Sift the dry ingredients into the bowl on top of the whisked
mixture. Gently mix so you don't knock out too much of the air
and pour the batter into the Swiss roll tin. Bake for 10–12 minutes
until springy to touch.

4 Once ready, remove from the oven and carefully lift the cake
from the tin by holding the parchment. Roll the cake up tightly
in the paper from the shortest end and leave to cool completely.

5 For the maple cream filling, whisk the cream, maple syrup
and vanilla until creamy and pillowy.

6 Unroll the cold cake and spread the filling all over the base.

7 Roll the cake back up, pulling the paper off as you go, and
place onto a cake board or plate.

8 Trim the ends to neaten and sprinkle with a dusting of
icing sugar.

Tips
Rolling the cake up as soon as it
comes out from the oven stops it
from cracking.

For the pumpkin purée, I sliced a
pumpkin in half, scooped out the
seeds and roasted it cut side down
in a hot oven. Once cool enough to
handle, I scooped out the flesh and
blitzed it to a purée. You can also
buy tinned pumpkin purée if
you prefer.

Carrot-top pesto oven-baked sandwich

YOU WILL NEED A FOOD PROCESSOR & A BAKING SHEET

————

I love pesto, especially when it's made with the carrot tops from
our homegrown carrots – perfect for adding to sandwiches, pasta, pizza or
as a dip. This baked sandwich topped with pesto is delicious and makes a
quick lunch with some roasted tomatoes on the vine.

MAKES 1 SANDWICH

For the carrot-top pesto

120g/4oz carrot tops
15g/½oz basil
50g/1½oz mix of pine nuts and
   pumpkin seeds
55g/2oz Parmesan, grated
2 garlic cloves
2 tbsp lemon juice
60ml/2fl oz olive oil
Salt and pepper, to taste

For the sandwich

2 slices of thick stale bread
Butter
Filling of choice
   (I use ham and cheese)
1 large egg
40ml/1½fl oz double cream
Salt and pepper

1   For the pesto, remove the tough stalks and stems from the
carrot tops, rinse well and drain, then use a paper towel to remove
excess moisture.

2   Place the carrot tops, basil, pine nuts, pumpkin seeds, grated
parmesan and garlic in a food processor and blitz, adding the
lemon juice, then the oil little by little. Season with a little salt
and pepper to taste if you wish.

3   Preheat the oven to 210°C (190°C fan oven) Gas 6.

4   Butter the bread, and make a sandwich with your chosen
filling and a little pesto.

5   In a bowl, lightly beat the egg, mix with cream and season
with salt and pepper.

6   Place the sandwich into the bowl to soak up the creamy
mixture, then flip. (Stale bread will absorb more of the mix.)

7   Lay a sheet of baking parchment on the worktop and place the
sandwich on top. Pour the remaining mixture over it and add a
large dollop of pesto to the top.

8   Wrap up the sandwich in parchment and tuck the ends
underneath. Bake for 30–40 minutes.

Tip
I often make a big batch of pesto
by doubling or tripling the
ingredients, then popping into
ice cube trays and freezing it.
The pesto will also keep in the
fridge for around a week.

Cake crumb cookies

YOU WILL NEED A FOOD PROCESSOR & A BAKING SHEET

When levelling cakes, there are always the leftover bits, which I must admit I eat as baker's perks, but sometimes it's nice to turn them into something else! Would you believe that you can make cookies out of crumbs? For this recipe I use chocolate cake crumbs, but experiment with whatever cake you have.

MAKES 20 COOKIES

For the cookies
150g/5oz leftover chocolate cake
90g/3oz honey roasted peanuts
Pinch of fine salt
½ tsp bicarbonate of soda
150g/5oz plain flour
115g/4oz unsalted butter
180g/6½oz soft brown sugar
1 tsp vanilla bean paste
1 large egg, beaten

To decorate
50g/1½oz chocolate drops
Coarse sea salt

1   Blitz the leftover cake and half the nuts in a food processor and add to a bowl along with the salt, bicarbonate of soda, flour and the remaining whole nuts.

2   Beat the butter, sugar and vanilla in a bowl until smooth, then add the beaten egg.

3   Mix the dry ingredients into the wet ingredients and place the bowl into the fridge to chill.

4   Once the dough has firmed up, weigh it and divide into 20 equal pieces. Roll each piece into a ball and pop back in the fridge.

5   Preheat the oven to 210°C (190°C fan oven) Gas 6. Space the balls of dough on a baking sheet and then bake for 8–10 minutes. Transfer them to a cooling rack to cool.

6   To decorate, melt the chocolate drops in a heatproof bowl in the microwave in 15-second bursts until melted and smooth. Alternatively, melt the chocolate in a bowl over a pan of simmering water.

7   Drizzle melted chocolate over the cookies when cooled and scatter with a little sea salt.

Mini mushroom quiches

YOU WILL NEED 6 X 10CM/4IN LOOSE-BOTTOMED TART TINS

These little tarts are so flavoursome! We grew the mushrooms on our windowsill
using a mushroom kit – they were so easy and fun to grow.

MAKES 6 SMALL TARTS

For the pastry
250g/9oz plain flour
125g/4½oz unsalted butter
20g/½oz Cheddar cheese,
    finely grated
2–3 tbsp cold milk

Or 1 sheet of ready-rolled
    shortcrust pastry

For the filling
1 small onion
Knob of butter
1 clove of garlic
1 tbsp wholegrain mustard
1 tbsp chopped parsley
300g/10½oz mushrooms
45g/1½oz Cheddar cheese
1 large egg
130ml/4½fl oz double cream
Salt and pepper

1   To make the pastry, place the flour and butter in a large bowl
and rub together to resemble fine breadcrumbs. Add the finely
grated cheese and then the milk a tablespoon at a time, until the
pastry comes together. Alternatively, you can make this the same
way using a food processor, and pulse until the dough comes
together to form a ball.

2   Shape the pastry into a disc, wrap it in baking parchment and
leave in the fridge to firm up for 20 minutes.

3   Meanwhile, make the filling. Finely chop the onion and add to
a pan with the butter. Crush the garlic clove into the pan and cook
until soft. Add the mustard and parsley, then the mushrooms.
Cook for a further 5 minutes and leave to cool.

4   Preheat the oven to 220°C (200°C fan oven) Gas 7.

5   Weigh the dough and divide it into six pieces. Working with
one at a time, roll the pastry out slightly larger than the tin. Lift
the pastry into the tin and press it into the base and up the sides,
leaving a slight overhang over the edge of the tin. Continue until
all six tins are lined, then place the tins onto a baking sheet.

6   Prick the base of each tart with a fork, line the cases with
greaseproof paper and fill with baking beans. Bake the pastry
cases for 10 minutes, then remove the beans and paper and bake
for 10 minutes more. Trim the overhanging edges of pastry with
a sharp knife or vegetable peeler, and leave to cool.

7   Lower the oven temperature to 180°C (160°C fan oven) Gas 4.

8   Grate the cheese into the mushroom mixture and divide
between the six mini tins, reserving a few mushrooms for the top.

9   Whisk the egg and cream together in a jug and season with a
little salt and pepper. Pour the creamy mixture into the tart cases
and top with the reserved mushrooms.

10 Bake for 20–25 minutes until lightly golden and the middle
still has a slight wobble.

Tip
The best quiche jiggles a little
when you cut into it and is silky
and creamy, so don't be tempted
to overbake.

Pumpkin cupcakes

YOU WILL NEED A BAKING SHEET, A 12-HOLE CUPCAKE TIN & PAPER CASES,
A PIPING BAG & ROUND NOZZLE

These super moist pumpkin cupcakes are easy to make, perfectly spiced and finished with a tangy citrusy cream cheese frosting – and topped with cute little meringue ghosts!

MAKES 12 CUPCAKES

For the cupcakes
220g/7½oz pumpkin purée
   (see p.114)
100ml/3½fl oz vegetable oil
2 large eggs
1 tsp vanilla bean paste
150g/5oz plain flour
1 tsp baking powder
100g/3½oz golden caster sugar
1 tsp ground cinnamon
½ tsp ground ginger
½ tsp ground nutmeg

For the cream cheese frosting
115g/4oz unsalted butter
360g/12½oz icing sugar
225g/8oz full fat cream cheese
1 tsp ground cinnamon
Zest of 1 orange
¼ tsp vanilla bean paste
Orange food gel

For the meringue ghosts
2 large egg whites
160g/5½oz caster sugar
Black edible pen

Sprinkles, to decorate

Tips
Keep the pumpkin seeds and toss in a little oil and paprika and roast for a tasty healthy snack!

Meringue kisses will keep well in an airtight container for around 2 weeks.

1 To make the meringue ghosts, start by preheating the oven to 120°C (100°C fan oven) Gas ½.

2 In a grease-free bowl of a stand mixer, whisk the egg whites until foamy and doubled in size. Add the sugar a spoonful at a time, until all the sugar is used up, the meringue is thick, glossy and holds stiff peaks and you can no longer feel sugar grains when you rub a little of the mixture between your fingers. Place a round piping nozzle into a piping bag and add the meringue.

3 Use a little meringue mixture in each corner to stick baking parchment to a baking sheet, then pipe shapes by gently squeezing the meringue onto the paper, pulling away slowly to make a peak.

4 Bake for 30–40 minutes until dry to touch and they peel away easily from the paper. Leave to cool. When dry, draw some eyes and an open mouth onto the meringues with an edible pen to look like little ghosts.

5 To make the cupcakes, preheat the oven to 190°C (170°C fan oven) Gas 5 and line a cupcake tin with 12 paper cases.

6 Whisk the pumpkin purée, oil, eggs and vanilla together in a jug.

7 In a large bowl, add the flour, baking powder, sugar and spices together, then pour in the wet ingredients and mix well. Spoon the batter into the cupcake cases, filling them three-quarters full, and bake for 20 minutes or until a skewer comes out clean when poked into the middle. Remove from the tin and place onto a cooling rack to cool.

8 For the cream cheese frosting, beat the butter until light and soft and add the icing sugar. Beat until smooth, then add the cream cheese, cinnamon, zest and vanilla. Add orange food gel and mix well.

9 Snip the end off a piping bag and push a round piping nozzle into the end. Fill the bag with the frosting and pipe a large swirl on top of each cupcake. Decorate with colourful sprinkles if you like and add the meringue ghosts.

Chocolate, almond & caramel babka

YOU WILL NEED A 900G/2 LB LOAF TIN

———

A babka is a sweet braided enriched bread with a
super chocolatey filling. I've taken this one a step further by adding
caramel and nuts to make it even more indulgent!

CUTS INTO 8–10 SLICES

For the dough
280g/10oz plain flour
30g/1oz golden caster sugar
¼ tsp fine salt
7g sachet fast-action yeast
55ml/2fl oz whole milk, warmed
2 medium eggs, beaten
85g/3oz unsalted butter, plus extra
    for greasing
Olive oil, for greasing

For the filling
70g/2½oz unsalted butter
55g/2oz chocolate drops
100g/3½oz golden caster sugar
40g/1½oz cocoa powder
100g/3½oz caramel
60g/2oz blanched almonds
½ tsp flaky sea salt

For the syrup
80g/3oz caster sugar
80ml/3fl oz water

1   For the dough, put the flour in the bowl of a stand mixer and add the sugar, the salt to one side and the yeast to the other. Make a well in the centre and add the lukewarm milk and beaten eggs. Start the mixer, using a dough hook, and add the butter a little at a time. Continue mixing until the dough is soft and elastic.

2   Lightly oil a large bowl with a little olive oil and place the dough in the bowl, cover with a clean damp tea towel and leave to double in size.

3   Once the dough has risen, knock it back by pushing the air out.

4   For the filling, melt the butter in a saucepan over a low heat, then add the chocolate drops and sugar and mix well until smooth. Add the cocoa powder, tip into a bowl and set to one side to cool.

5   Lightly grease the loaf tin and line the base and sides with baking parchment, leaving the paper overhanging as this will make it easier to lift the baked babka out later.

6   Lightly flour a worktop and roll out the dough into a rectangle approximately 30 x 40cm/12 x 16in. Carefully smooth the chocolate filling all over the dough, leaving a small border around the edge. Spoon over the caramel in stripes using a spoon or piping bag, then scatter with the almonds and sea salt.

7   Roll up the dough tightly from the longest end, with the seam facing downwards. Score a line down the centre across the length of the dough as a guide, then cut all the way through so you have two long pieces.

8   Turn the pieces so the cut side is facing upwards, then lay them out in an X shape. Keeping the cut sides facing upwards, twist the two pieces together. Pinch the ends of the twist together to seal, tucking the ends under. Carefully lift the dough into the prepared tin, cover with a clean damp tea towel and leave to double in size.

9 Preheat your oven to 200°C (180°C fan oven) Gas 6, and bake the babka for 10 minutes. Reduce the temperature to 170°C (150°C fan oven) Gas 3 and bake for a further 20–25 minutes until golden brown. If you find the babka browning too quickly, cover the top with foil and continue to bake.

10 While the babka is baking, place the sugar and water into a small saucepan and heat to dissolve the sugar, then turn up the heat and keep stirring until you have a thick syrup.

11 Once the babka is ready, place the tin on a cooling rack and brush the hot babka with the sugar syrup. Sprinkle with a little sea salt if you like, then when the babka is cool enough to handle, lift it out using the baking paper, leave to cool completely and slice.

Cookies 'hawdd'

————

'Hawdd' means 'easy' in Welsh, so we named these cookies 'hawdd'
in our house as they are just that! I make big batches of the mixture, roll it into
balls and freeze. If unexpected visitors pop round, the cookies can be baked from
frozen in the time it takes to boil the kettle! My son loves to sandwich toasted
marshmallows or ice cream between these cookies too!

MAKES 16 COOKIES

120g/4oz unsalted butter
160g/5½oz caster sugar
1 large egg, beaten
1 tsp vanilla bean paste
180g/6½oz plain flour
1 tsp baking powder
½ tsp fine salt
170g/6oz chocolate drops

1   Beat the butter and sugar together in a bowl until light and fluffy.

2   Add the beaten egg and vanilla, then add the flour, baking powder and salt. Mix together well, then add the chocolate drops and mix to distribute evenly.

3   Bring the dough together into a rough ball, weigh the mix and divide into 16 pieces.

4   Preheat the oven to 210°C (190°C fan oven) Gas 6.

5   Roll each piece into a ball and place on a baking tray, leaving gaps in between as they will spread while baking. Alternatively, you can freeze them at this stage.

6   Bake for 8–10 minutes, then leave to cool on the baking sheet for 5 minutes before transferring to a cooling rack. The cookies will be soft in the centre, but they will firm up as they cool.

Pear and ginger Viennese whirls

YOU WILL NEED BAKING SHEETS, A PIPING BAG & STAR NOZZLE

————

I love making jars of pear and ginger jam at this time of the year,
using the ripe pears harvested from my Uncle Kev and Auntie Ron's pear tree.
What we don't eat, I turn into jam to enjoy all year round.

MAKES 12 SANDWICH BISCUITS

For the biscuits
250g/9oz unsalted butter
250g/9oz plain flour
50g/1½oz icing sugar
60g/2oz cornflour
1 tsp vanilla bean paste
½ tsp ground ginger

For the buttercream
150g/5oz unsalted butter
250g/9oz icing sugar
½ tsp vanilla bean paste
1–2 tbsp milk, to loosen

For the filling
Pear and Ginger Jam (see p.185)

Icing sugar, to dust

1   To make the biscuit dough, beat all the ingredients in a large bowl, or blitz in a food processor. Spoon the biscuit dough into a piping bag fitted with a large, open star nozzle and place it in the fridge for the dough to harden slightly. The dough needs to be soft enough to pipe but firm enough to hold its shape.

2   While the dough is chilling, preheat the oven to 190°C (170°C fan oven) Gas 5. Depending on the size of your trays, you may need to bake the biscuits in batches. Line each tray with baking parchment and draw around the base of a 4cm cookie cutter to make about eight circles on each sheet. You will have 24 biscuits in total. Flip the paper over so the ink doesn't transfer to the cookies.

3   Pipe circular swirls of mixture onto each sheet using the drawn circles as a template, finishing in the centre. Bake the biscuits for 10–12 minutes until they are a pale golden colour, then leave on the baking trays to harden slightly before moving onto a cooling rack to cool.

4   For the buttercream, beat the butter until light and fluffy, then add the icing sugar and beat well until pale in colour. Add the vanilla and enough milk to loosen.

5   Place the buttercream into a piping bag fitted with a star nozzle and pipe a swirl on the base of 12 biscuits.

6   Spoon 10–12 tsp of jam into a bowl and mix to loosen slightly. Spoon a teaspoon of jam onto the remaining 12 biscuits then sandwich them together, pressing gently so the filling comes to the edge. To finish, dust the biscuits with a little icing sugar.

Tip
Don't let a glut of fruit go to waste.
Fruits can be turned into jams and
curds to enjoy throughout the year.

Leek, cheese & black garlic pasties

YOU WILL NEED A BAKING SHEET

———

Craving comfort food? These cheesy leek pasties are the
perfect hearty snack and great straight from the oven. The black garlic
adds a sweet, earthy and mysterious taste!

MAKES 6 PASTIES

For the pastry
250g/9oz plain flour
125g/4½oz unsalted butter
20g/½oz Cheddar cheese,
    finely grated
2–3tbsp milk

For the filling
Knob of butter
1 small onion
1 small leek
80g/3oz mature Cheddar cheese
1 tbsp chopped fresh thyme
1½ tbsp Dijon mustard
1 tsp mustard seeds
5 peeled black garlic cloves

1 egg, to glaze
Nigella seeds

1   First, make the pastry. Place the flour and butter in a large
bowl and rub together until they resemble fine breadcrumbs.
Mix in the finely grated cheese and add the milk a tablespoon at a
time, until the pastry comes together. Alternatively, you can make
this the same way using a food processor, pulsing until the dough
comes together to form a ball.

2   Shape the pastry into a disc, wrap in baking parchment and
leave in the fridge to firm up for 20 minutes.

3   For the filling, melt a knob of butter in a frying pan and finely
chop the onion and leek. Soften the onion in the pan, then add
the leeks, cook briefly and then take off the heat and leave to cool.

4   In a bowl, coarsely grate the cheese, add the thyme, mustard
and mustard seeds, then mash the black garlic cloves with a fork
and add to the bowl. Stir in the cooled onions and leeks and leave
to cool completely.

5   Remove the pastry from the fridge and divide it into six pieces.
Roll out each piece to the thickness of a pound coin, and using
a cutter, stamp out six circles measuring 11cm/4½ in. Line two
baking sheets with parchment and place three pastry cutouts
onto each one.

6   Preheat the oven to 200°C (180°C fan oven) Gas 6.

7   Divide the onion mixture between the six pasties by spooning
over half of each circle.

8   Beat the egg and brush a little around the edges of the circles,
then fold the top half over the filling and crimp the edges to seal.

Brush all the pasties with the beaten egg and scatter over a few
nigella seeds. Using a sharp knife, make two little slits on the top
of each pasty and bake for 15–20 minutes until golden brown.

Bramble & bay glazed baked doughnuts

YOU WILL NEED A STAND MIXER & DOUGH HOOK, 2 BAKING SHEETS,
A DOUGHNUT CUTTER OR COOKIE CUTTER

———

Sweet treats don't come much sweeter than these delicious
baked doughnuts. The sweet and juicy taste of blackberries pairs beautifully
with the aromatic warmth of bay.

MAKES 12–14 DOUGHNUTS

For the dough
50g/1½oz unsalted butter
250ml/9fl oz whole milk
500g/1 lb 1½oz strong white
   bread flour
50g/1½oz caster sugar
2 tsp fine salt
14g (2 sachets) fast-action yeast
2 medium eggs
Olive oil, for greasing
   and brushing

For the glaze
100g/3½oz Blackberry and
   Bay Jam (see p.185)
300g/10½oz icing sugar
5 tsp water

Sprinkles or edible flowers,
   to decorate

1   To make the dough, place the butter and milk into a saucepan and gently heat until the butter has melted.

2   In the bowl of a stand mixer, place the flour and sugar, the salt to one side and yeast to the other, add the eggs, then slowly add the milky mixture and mix well, allowing the dough hook to knead the dough. This dough is very sticky so I find using the mixer a good idea!

3   Once the dough is smooth and elastic, lightly grease a bowl using a little olive oil, and pop the dough inside. Cover with a clean damp tea towel and leave to double in size.

4   Lightly grease two baking sheets with a little oil.

5   Roll out the dough onto a lightly floured surface to about 2cm/1in thick. Use a doughnut cutter or a cookie cutter to stamp out twelve doughnuts, re-rolling the dough as you go. Preheat the oven to 220°C (200°C fan oven) Gas 7.

6   Carefully lift the doughnuts onto a baking sheet and leave to rise, covering with a lightly oiled piece of cling film. The dough will be ready when it springs back slowly when you prod it.

7   Lightly brush the doughnuts with a little olive oil and bake for 8–10 minutes until lightly golden, then leave to cool on a cooling rack.

8   For the glaze, mix the jam with the icing sugar and enough water to make a thick icing. Dip the cooled doughnuts into the icing and leave to set. Decorate with sprinkles or edible flowers.

Tips
These are best eaten on the day once the icing has set.

You will find an abundance of blackberries this time of year in the hedgerows, so get picking!

Overnight Bircher

YOU WILL NEED A JAR OR POT

There's nothing healthier than eating overnight oats in the morning – it's the perfect way to start the day. Preparing this Bircher the night before allows the oats to soak up all those delicious flavours throughout the night, ready to top with fresh or frozen fruits and extra toppings the next morning.

MAKES 1 LARGE SERVING

1 banana
1 tbsp honey
1 tbsp peanut butter
1 tsp vanilla bean paste
½ tsp ground cinnamon
1 tbsp chia seeds
80g/3oz porridge oats
200ml/7fl oz nut milk/milk

To top
Fresh fruits
Granola
Peanut butter

1 Slice half the banana thinly and press the slices against the side of the jar, around the base.

2 Mash the rest of the banana in a bowl with the honey, peanut butter and vanilla. Add the cinnamon and chia seeds and mix well.

3 Add oats and milk into the mixture then pour into the jar.

4 Pop the lid on and leave in the fridge overnight.

5 In the morning, top with fresh fruits, granola and extra peanut butter.

Tip
Make sure you put the Bircher in a big enough pot, jar or tub so you have room to add extra toppings in the morning!

Tonka bean & blackberry baked cheesecake

YOU WILL NEED A 20CM/8IN ROUND LOOSE-BOTTOMED TIN

This creamy tonka bean baked cheesecake on a buttery, oaty biscuit base with sweet juicy blackberries is the perfect dinner party dessert.

SERVES 10

For the cheesecake
170g/6oz oat biscuits, e.g. Hobnobs
70g/2½oz unsalted butter, melted
635g/1 lb 6½oz full fat cream cheese
130g/4½oz caster sugar
100ml/3½fl oz double cream
3 large eggs, beaten
1 tsp vanilla bean paste
1 tonka bean

For the blackberry topping
200g/7oz fresh blackberries
3 tbsp water
3 tbsp caster sugar
3 tsp lemon juice

1 Preheat your oven to 160°C (140°C fan oven) Gas 3.

2 Whizz the biscuits to a fine crumb using a food processor, or alternatively you could place the biscuits in a sandwich bag and bash them with a rolling pin. Add the melted butter to the biscuits and mix well.

3 Tip the buttery biscuit mix into the bottom of the tin and, using the back of a spoon, press the base down firmly. Bake for 10 minutes. Leave the oven on at the same temperature.

4 For the filling, beat the cream cheese until fluffy, then add the sugar, cream, beaten eggs and vanilla. Grate over the tonka bean using a fine grater. Mix gently until smooth and pour onto the biscuit base.

5 Bake the cheesecake for 45–50 minutes; it will have a wobble in the centre. Turn off the heat and leave the cheesecake to cool in the oven.

6 Once cooled, place the cheesecake in the fridge overnight to firm up.

7 To make the topping, place the blackberries, water, sugar and lemon juice into a small saucepan and heat on a medium heat. Once the blackberries have started to soften, after around 10 minutes, remove them with a slotted spoon and leave to cool on a plate.

8 Reduce the syrup in the pan a little, depending on how thick you like it. The syrup will thicken as it cools.

9 To assemble, carefully remove the cheesecake from the tin and place onto a cake stand or plate. Pile the blackberries on top and drizzle over the syrup. Slice the cheesecake and top with extra syrup.

Tip
Don't overmix the cheesecake mixture as it may bubble and crack when baked.

———

Winter is a quiet time in the garden,

but I use the time to tidy up flower beds and borders,
make sure our water butts are working correctly ready to catch the
rainfall, and start thinking of bulbs and seeds I want to grow the
following year. I also start collecting egg boxes, egg shells,
toilet roll holders and yoghurt pots to use to sow seeds.
Some crops may need protection from the cold with fleece and
a cloche. I love curling up on the sofa this time of year and eating
comforting bakes, especially fruity crumble with custard!

What to plant

Although in the depths of winter you may not be able to grow much outside, I like to sow micro greens indoors and keep them on the windowsill to cut as we need them for a fresh, highly nutritious and flavourful sprinkling of greens. These can include alfalfa, fenugreek, red and green cabbage, beetroot, broccoli, amaranth, cress and chard but there are many more available. Don't worry if they start getting leggy due to lack of light; it won't affect the taste, just harvest them anyway.

What to harvest

Continue to harvest the summer and autumn crops such as leeks, kale, chard and winter lettuce. Now is a good time to prune fruit trees during the dormant season, including apples, pears, raspberries, blueberries and gooseberry bushes.

Tip

Make the most of the availability of Seville oranges. They only have a short season but have such a fragrant, fresh, intense flavour – perfect for cooking and even better as a marmalade. Check out my Seville Orange and Cinnamon Prinsesstårta Cake recipe on p.153 using Seville Orange Curd (p.186).

Chocolate loaf cake
with a hazelnut chocolate ganache
YOU WILL NEED A 900G/2 LB LOAF TIN

————

This simple chocolate loaf cake recipe is the perfect easy bake for new bakers. Chocolate and cake are two of my favourite things and this indulgent cake topped with hazelnut ganache definitely hits the spot.

SERVES 8–10

For the cake

180g/6½oz unsalted butter, plus extra for greasing

180g/6½oz caster sugar

3 eggs, beaten

55g/2oz cocoa powder

2 tsp instant coffee mixed with 50ml/1½fl oz boiling water

1½ tsp vanilla bean paste

180g/6½oz plain flour

½ tsp baking powder

2–3 tbsp milk

For the hazelnut ganache

100g/3½oz chocolate drops

150g/5oz Nutella chocolate hazelnut spread

240ml/8½fl oz double cream

Chopped roasted hazelnuts, to decorate

1 Preheat the oven to 170°C (150°C fan oven) Gas 3. Grease and line the loaf tin, allowing the paper to overhang the edges.

2 In a bowl, beat the butter until light and fluffy, then add the sugar and beat until smooth. Add the beaten eggs. Mix the cocoa powder with the coffee and water in a small bowl and add the vanilla. Pour into the larger bowl and mix well.

3 Add the flour and baking powder to the bowl and mix well. Add enough milk to loosen the batter, then pour into the prepared tin and bake for 50–55 minutes or until a skewer comes out clean.

4 Leave the cake to cool in the tin for 10 minutes, then using the parchment, lift the loaf cake out of the tin and leave to cool completely on a cooling rack.

5 For the ganache, put the chocolate drops in a bowl along with the Nutella spread. Pour the cream into a small saucepan and heat until steaming. Pour the cream straight on the chocolate and Nutella and mix until completely melted. Leave to cool; the mixture will thicken as it cools.

6 Once the cake has cooled, top with ganache and use a palette knife to create swirls in the chocolate. Top with a few chopped roasted hazelnuts.

Spiced carrot & pumpkin Bundt cake

YOU WILL NEED A BUNDT TIN

———

I absolutely love a Bundt cake and have quite a collection of tins.
The tin does the hard work for you by giving your bakes an impressive shape.
The way the frosting runs down the grooves on this spiced cake is simply
beautiful and will give you the wow factor.

SERVES 12

For the cake
80g/3oz sultanas
Zest and juice of 1 orange
140g/5oz carrots
300g/10½oz caster sugar
6 large eggs
300ml/11fl oz vegetable oil
125g/4½oz pumpkin purée
100g/3½oz chopped pecans
Pinch of salt
4 tsp ground cinnamon
3 tsp ground mixed spice
1½ tsp bicarbonate of soda
300g/10½oz plain flour, plus
 extra for dusting
Melted butter, for greasing

For the cream cheese frosting
100g/3½oz unsalted butter, softened
190g/6½oz icing sugar
Zest of 1 orange
90g/3oz full fat cream cheese
1½ tsp ground cinnamon
3–4 tbsp milk

Edible flowers, to decorate
 (optional)

1 Preheat the oven to 190°C (170°C fan oven) Gas 5. Grease a Bundt tin well with a little melted butter and dust the inside with a little flour.

2 Place the sultanas in a microwavable bowl along with the orange juice and zest, heat for 1½ minutes and allow to cool. Grate the carrots and set to one side.

3 Whisk the sugar, eggs and oil together in a large bowl, then add the grated carrots and pumpkin purée.

4 Add the chopped pecans to the bowl along with the salt, spices and bicarbonate of soda, add the flour and mix well. Add the sultanas and remaining juice to the bowl, and mix to combine. Pour into the tin and bake for 40–50 minutes or until a skewer comes out clean. Leave the tin to cool on a cooling rack for 10 minutes, then turn the cake out gently and leave to cool.

5 For the cream cheese frosting, beat the softened butter and icing sugar until smooth. Add orange zest, then the cream cheese, then beat. Add the cinnamon and enough milk to loosen the frosting so it will drip slightly once it's poured onto the cake.

6 When the cake is cool, pour the frosting over the top so it drips slightly into the crevices. Decorate with a few edible petals.

Open-top mince pies

YOU WILL NEED A BAKING SHEET

———

Leading up to Christmas, you'll always find a batch of these
under a cloche in my kitchen! They are light, super easy to make and
have the taste of Christmas in every bite.

MAKES 12

For the mince pies
12 tsp mincemeat
Zest of 1 orange
2 tbsp rum (optional)
30g/1oz dried chopped cranberries
3 tbsp ground almonds
Rough puff pastry (see p.62) or
   1 sheet ready-rolled puff pastry

To decorate
15g/½oz chopped pecans
15g/½oz chopped pistachios
Icing sugar, to dust

1 beaten egg, to glaze
Demerara sugar, to sprinkle

1   Preheat the oven to 200°C (180°C fan oven) Gas 6.

2   Put the mincemeat, zest, rum, cranberries and ground almonds in a bowl and mix together well.

3   Line two baking sheets with baking parchment. Unroll the pastry (or roll out your rough puff to 23 x 35cm/9 x 14in) and cut it into 12 equal squares. Place six pieces of pastry on each sheet and push a circle cutter into the middle of each square, but not right the way through.

4   Add a couple of teaspoons of filling inside each stamped circle. Do not overfill as the mixture will spread as they bake.

5   Brush the edges of the pastry with the beaten egg wash, then sprinkle with a little demerara sugar.

6   Bake for 15 minutes, and once baked transfer to a cooling rack and top with chopped nuts.

7   When they have cooled a little, dust with icing sugar.

Tip
I love popping these into cute little gift bags tied with pretty ribbon and sharing them with friends and family over the festive period

Mini gingerbread cheesecakes

YOU WILL NEED A 12-HOLE CUPCAKE TIN & PAPER CASES, A PIPING BAG & STAR NOZZLE

If you're a fan of cheesecake, you'll love these. My irresistible, creamy
no-bake mini cheesecakes with a crunchy base are loaded with delightful
gingerbread flavours and are the perfect seasonal treat!

MAKES 12

For the base
250g/9oz gingerbread biscuits
150g/5oz unsalted butter, melted

For the filling
600g/1lb 5oz full fat cream cheese
80g/3oz soft brown sugar
60g/2oz icing sugar
40g/1½oz black treacle
1 tsp vanilla bean paste
2 tsp cinnamon
2 tsp mixed spice
2½ tsp ground ginger
300ml/11fl oz double cream

To decorate
300ml/11fl oz double cream
Ginger syrup
Few blitzed gingerbread
    biscuit crumbs

1 Line a cupcake tin with paper cases.

2 Blitz the biscuits in a food processor or place the biscuits in
a bag and bash with a rolling pin. Tip the biscuit crumbs into a
bowl, add the melted butter and mix together.

3 Divide the biscuit crumbs between the paper cases and firmly
press into the base of each one using the bottom of a small glass,
then pop the tin into the fridge.

4 For the filling, whisk the cream cheese, sugars, treacle, vanilla
and spices together until smooth. Add the cream then whisk until
thick.

5 Remove the tin from the fridge and top the biscuit bases with
the cheesecake mixture, smoothing the tops with a palette knife.
Pop the cheesecakes back into the fridge to firm up for a few
hours, or preferably overnight.

6 When ready to serve, whip up the cream until soft and pillowy,
then spoon into a piping bag fitted with a star nozzle and pipe
a little swirl on top of each cheesecake.

7 Drizzle the tops with the ginger syrup and scatter over a few
biscuit crumbs.

Tips
Using full fat cream cheese helps
the cheesecakes set well.

These will keep for 4–5 days in
the fridge.

Seville orange & cinnamon prinsesstårta cake

YOU WILL NEED A 20CM/8IN ROUND CAKE TIN, PIPING BAGS, ROUND NOZZLE & STAR NOZZLE

I make this Swedish layer cake every year for my husband's birthday
as it's his favourite cake ever, but I switch up the flavours and colours each time.
This cake has it all: layers of light and airy sponge, cinnamon custard, tangy
Seville orange curd and whipped cream, all encased in a layer of sweet,
nutty marzipan. It's the perfect celebration cake.

SERVES 12

For the cinnamon custard
300ml/11fl oz whole milk
1 tsp vanilla bean paste
2 tsp ground cinnamon
3 egg yolks
50g/1½oz caster sugar
30g/1oz cornflour
30g/1oz unsalted butter

Seville Orange Curd (see p.186)

For the sponge
5 large eggs
165g/6oz caster sugar
165g/6oz plain flour
40g/1½oz unsalted butter, melted,
    plus extra for greasing

For the filling, sides and top
600ml/1pt 1fl oz double cream

For the marzipan
200g/7oz ground almonds
75g/2½oz caster sugar
125g/4½oz icing sugar, plus
    extra for dusting
1 medium egg, beaten
1 tsp almond extract
Orange food colouring

To decorate
150ml/5½fl oz double cream
Dried orange slices and pine
    cones (optional)

1 For the custard, pour the milk into a small pan with the vanilla and ground cinnamon and place over a low heat for 2–3 minutes until just simmering. Remove from the heat and set aside.

2 In a large bowl, whisk the egg yolks, sugar and cornflour together until pale and creamy.

3 Strain the milk through a sieve into a jug, then slowly pour onto the egg mixture, mixing with a whisk until smooth.

4 Pour the mixture back into the pan and cook over a low heat for 4–5 minutes, whisking continuously until very thick. Remove from the heat and beat in the butter, then transfer to a bowl and cover the surface with cling film to prevent a skin forming. Leave to cool then pop into the fridge to chill.

5 Preheat your oven to 180°C (160°C fan oven) Gas 4 and line and grease the base and sides of the cake tin.

6 To make the sponge, whisk the eggs and sugar in a stand mixer until the mixture is mousse-like and leaves a ribbon when you lift the whisk. Gently sift the flour over the mixture in three additions, gently folding after each time with a large metal spoon. Slowly add the butter down the side of the bowl, taking care not to overmix.

7 Carefully pour the mixture into the prepared tin and bake for 20–25 minutes until the sponge is golden, then leave to cool in the tin for 10 minutes before turning out onto a wire rack to cool.

8 Once the cake has cooled, cut the sponge horizontally into three thin even layers.

9 Place one sponge layer onto a cake stand, and spread a thin layer of the custard over the base.

10 Place a quarter of the custard into a piping bag fitted with a round nozzle and pipe a border around the edge of the sponge, approximately 1cm/½in in from the side. Spoon 5–6 tbsp of the curd inside the 'wall' and smooth with a palette knife.

11 Whip the double cream until firm and fold half into the remaining custard. Put the rest to one side for now.

12 Spread a third of the custard cream mixture on top of the curd layer, place the next sponge on top, then spread over the remaining custard cream.

13 Place the final sponge on top, then cover the sides with a thin layer of the whipped double cream set aside from earlier. Pile the rest of the cream on top of the cake and use a palette knife to shape into a dome shape. Place the cake in the fridge to set.

14 Meanwhile, to make the marzipan, mix the ground almonds and sugars together in a stand mixer. Add the beaten egg and almond extract and mix to form a stiff dough. Mix in a little food colouring, then roll out on a surface lightly dusted with icing sugar to a circle about 40cm/16in in diameter, large enough to cover the whole cake.

15 Remove the cake from the fridge. Lift the marzipan up over the cake, using the rolling pin to help, and smooth down the sides to get a smooth finish. Trim away any excess from the base.

16 Whip the 150ml of double cream until pillowy, then put it into a piping bag fitted with a small star nozzle. Pipe small stars of cream all around the base and decorate with dried orange slices and pinecones.

Festive stollen couronne

YOU WILL NEED A BAKING SHEET & A PIPING BAG (OPTIONAL)

———

This enriched sweet bread is packed with plump, juicy fruits laced with alcohol,
with nuggets of sweet marzipan running through the middle.

SERVES 10–12

For the dough
150ml/5½fl oz whole milk
50g/1½oz soft unsalted butter
300g/10½oz strong white bread flour
40g/1½oz caster sugar
1 tsp salt
7g sachet fast-action yeast
1 large egg, beaten
Olive oil, for greasing

For the filling
190g/6½oz mixed dried fruit of
    your choice (I use a mixture
    of apricots, glacé cherries,
    cranberries, sultanas, raisins
    and mixed peel)
80ml/3fl oz alcohol/orange juice
    (I use amaretto)
90g/3oz unsalted butter
90g/3oz soft brown sugar
1 tsp vanilla bean paste
60g/2oz chopped nuts (I use
    flaked almonds)
Zest of 1 orange
20g/½oz ground almonds
60g/2oz marzipan, grated

To decorate
3 tbsp apricot jam
3 tbsp icing sugar
Juice of 1 orange
Flaked almonds

1 For the filling, place the dried fruit in a bowl with the alcohol, cover with a tea towel and leave overnight to plump up.

2 To make the dough, heat the milk and butter in a saucepan over a low heat until just warm and the butter has melted.

3 Place the flour and sugar in a bowl, add the salt on one side and the yeast on the other. Make a well in the centre, add the milk mixture and roughly mix together, adding the beaten egg. Keep mixing together until the dough forms a ball, then knead on the worktop until smooth and elastic. You can also make this in a stand mixer fitted with a dough hook. The dough will be sticky but don't be tempted to add more flour.

4 Once the dough is smooth and silky, leave it to prove in a lightly oiled bowl, covered with a clean damp tea towel, until doubled in size. To make the filling, beat the butter and sugar with the vanilla until light and fluffy, add the nuts, zest and ground almonds and mix well. Strain any liquid from the fruits, then stir the fruit into the mix. Grate the marzipan and set to one side. Line a baking sheet with parchment paper.

5 Once the dough is ready, knock the air out gently and, on a lightly floured surface, shape it into a large rectangle approximately 25 x 35cm/10 x 14in.

6 Spread the fruity mixture evenly on top of the dough leaving a 2cm/1in border around the perimeter. Scatter grated marzipan all over. Roll the dough up tightly from the longest end and trim the ends to neaten. Using a sharp knife, cut right through the middle of the dough lengthways, leaving one end attached slightly.

7 Twist the two pieces over each other to form a wreath shape, tucking the ends underneath to seal. Carefully lift the wreath onto the tray and leave to prove until doubled in size, covering with a piece of cling film or a proving bag. I often put a small cookie cutter into the centre of the wreath, so when the dough rises you still have a good shape.

8 Heat your oven to 210°C (190°C fan oven) Gas 6. When the dough has risen, bake for 30–40 minutes until golden brown. (If you notice the dough browning too quickly, cover with foil.) Remove the wreath from the oven and slide it straight onto a cooling rack. Mix the apricot jam with a little water and heat in the microwave for a few seconds. Brush the warm wreath with the jam and leave to cool completely.

9 For the icing, mix the icing sugar with a little juice from the orange to make a thick paste. Spread a little icing all over the wreath using a piping bag or a small spoon. Scatter the top with a few flaked almonds to decorate.

Maple & pecan banana bread

YOU WILL NEED A 900G/2 LB LOAF TIN

Banana bread seemed to be everyone's favourite during lockdown
and so many people got involved with baking. This one is a favourite of mine
as it's indulgent, sticky and extremely moreish, plus it's a great way to use
up those bananas from the fruit bowl that are past their best.

SERVES 8–10

3 ripe bananas
125g/4½oz unsalted butter,
   plus extra for greasing
160g/5½oz golden caster sugar
2 large eggs, beaten
120g/4oz plain flour
120g/4oz wholemeal flour
1 tsp baking powder
1 tsp ground cinnamon
40ml/1½fl oz maple syrup
1 tsp vanilla bean paste
60g/2oz pecans, roughly chopped

Maple syrup, to drizzle

1 Preheat the oven to 180°C (160°C fan oven) Gas 4. Lightly grease the tin and line it with baking parchment.

2 Mash two of the bananas with a fork and slice the other in half lengthways.

3 Beat the butter and sugar together until light and creamy, add the beaten eggs, flours, baking powder and cinnamon then briefly mix.

4 Add the maple syrup, vanilla and the mashed banana. Stir through the roughly chopped pecans and pour the mixture into the prepared tin. Lay the sliced banana on top with the cut side facing upwards. Bake for around an hour or until a skewer comes out clean.

5 Once baked, place the tin on a cooling rack and drizzle the loaf with a little maple syrup. Leave to cool slightly, then remove from the tin and leave to cool completely.

Tips

Ripe bananas make the best banana bread; the blacker they are the sweeter the taste!

Don't overmix the batter; the more you do the more chewy and rubbery your cake will be.

Butternut squash, feta, maple & pecan cups

YOU WILL NEED A 12-HOLE CUPCAKE TIN

I'm going to be totally honest: I've never made my own filo pastry.
I must try one day. This recipe uses shop-bought pastry and these roasted
vegetable cups are deliciously crisp and full of flavour.

MAKES 12

1 large butternut squash
2 shallots
3 sprigs fresh rosemary
2 tbsp vegetable oil
3 tbsp maple syrup
Salt and pepper, to taste
80g/3oz pecans, chopped
1 pack filo pastry
100g/3½oz butter, melted,
    plus extra for greasing
100g/3½oz feta cheese, crumbled

1 Preheat the oven to 200°C (180°C fan oven) Gas 6.

2 Start by peeling and deseeding the butternut squash, then cut it into small chunks. Roughly chop the shallots and place both in an ovenproof dish along with the chopped rosemary.

3 Mix the oil with the maple syrup and pour on top of the vegetables. Add a little salt and pepper and toss all together, coating well. Roast in the oven for 40–50 minutes, add the chopped pecans, mix well then leave to cool.

4 Meanwhile, unroll the filo pastry and cut into equal quarters, cutting through all the layers at the same time.

5 Grease each hole of the tin with a little butter. Brush one square of pastry with a little melted butter, top with another piece, then continue with two more pieces in the same way. (Keep the remaining pastry under a clean damp tea towel as you work to stop it drying out.)

6 Push the buttered squares into one of the holes, then carry on with the rest until all the holes are lined. If you have any leftover squares of pastry, add them to the others.

7 Fill each cup with the filling, sprinkle with the feta cheese and bake for 15–20 minutes until the pastry is golden and crunchy.

8 Carefully lift out each pastry cup from the tin and serve warm.

Tip
Don't throw away the seeds from the squash! Rinse them, pat dry and coat in a little olive oil, salt and a few fennel seeds. Roast in the oven until they start to pop – a little tasty snack!

Festive tiffin

YOU WILL NEED A 20CM/8IN SQUARE TIN

————

I often make tiffin to use up the leftover odds and ends of chocolate, biscuits, fruits and nuts that we have lying around. Making two different flavoured tiffins in one tin at the same time gives people a choice of which one they fancy – or if you're like me, you can have one of each!

MAKES 12–16 SQUARES

For the base
200g/7oz ginger biscuits
50g/1½oz pistachios
60g/2oz dried cranberries
45g/1½oz dried chopped apricots
20g/½oz chopped crystallised ginger
4 tsp mixed peel
125g/4½oz butter, plus extra for greasing
2 tbsp golden syrup
250g/9oz white chocolate drops
250g/9oz milk chocolate drops

For the ganache topping
60g/2oz white chocolate drops
60g/2oz milk chocolate drops
120ml/4fl oz double cream
1 tbsp rum (optional)
10 drops of pina colada flavouring (optional)

To decorate
Dried edible flowers
Desiccated coconut

Tip
Don't chop the fillings too small as it's great to have crunchy and juicy pieces in each bite.

1 Lightly grease the tin and line the base and sides with baking parchment. Cut a piece of foil the same width as the tin, then fold it a couple of times so it is thick and sturdy but keeping its length. Lightly grease the foil and cover with a piece of baking parchment. This will go into the centre of the tin to make two different flavoured tiffins.

2 Roughly chop the biscuits and nuts and put in a bowl along with the fruit, ginger and mixed peel.

3 Melt the butter and golden syrup in a bowl over a pan of simmering water. Place the chocolate drops in separate bowls, milk in one and white in the other, and equally divide the butter mixture between the bowls. Mix well to melt the chocolate. (Don't worry if it goes a little grainy or separates, just add a little boiled water bit by bit until it comes back smooth and runny.)

4 Equally divide the biscuit, nut and fruit mix between the bowls and mix well. Place your foil divider in the middle of the tin and tip the milk chocolate mixture to one side and the white to the other. Press them flat into the tin using the back of a spoon and pop in the fridge to firm up slightly.

5 Meanwhile, make the ganache. Place the white chocolate drops in one bowl and milk in the other.

6 Heat the cream in a small saucepan until steaming, take off the heat and divide it equally between the two bowls of chocolate. Stir until melted, then, if using, add rum to the milk chocolate ganache and the pina colada drops to the white. Leave to cool until just warm.

7 When the tiffin has firmed up, pour the milk chocolate ganache over the darker base and the white chocolate ganache on the white one, then leave in the fridge until firm (preferably overnight).

8 Remove the tin from the fridge, lift the tiffin out and cut into equal squares. Add dried pressed flowers to the top of the slices and sprinkle a little desiccated coconut to the white chocolate tiffin to pretty them up!

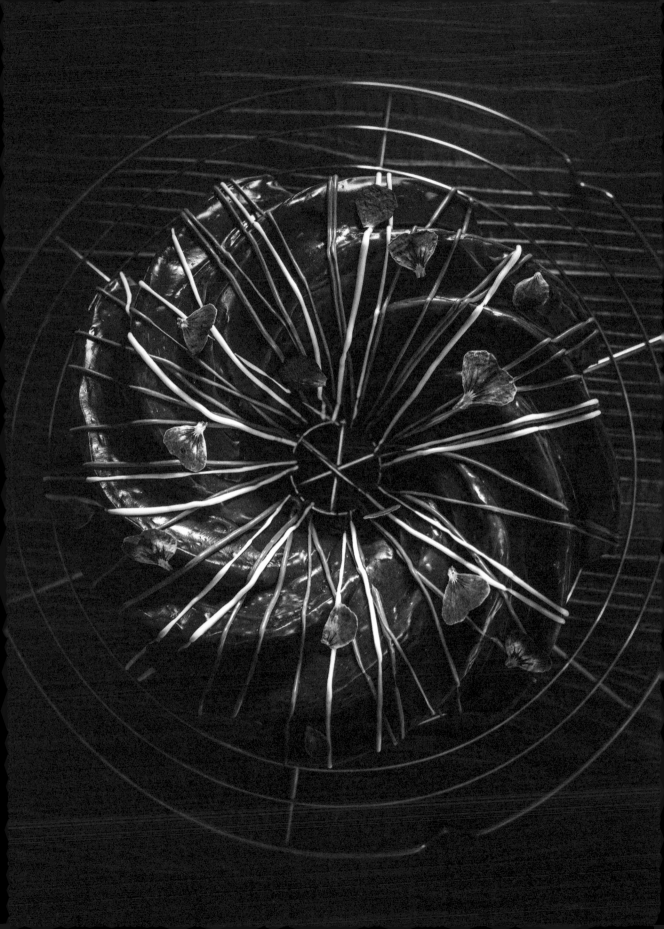

Marbled Bundt cake

YOU WILL NEED A BUNDT TIN

————

Marble cake is one of the first things I baked on my own from the cookbook
I bought as a child from the touring bus library that came to my school, so every time
I make this two-toned cake it takes me back to fond childhood memories.

SERVES 12

For the cake
190g/6½oz unsalted butter,
   plus extra for greasing
240g/8½oz golden caster sugar
3 large eggs
190g/6½oz plain flour, plus
   extra for dusting
1½ tsp baking powder
80g/3oz ground almonds
1½ tsp almond extract
½ tsp vanilla bean paste
1–2 tbsp milk
Purple food gel

For the ganache
200ml/7fl oz double cream
200g/7oz milk chocolate drops

To decorate
60g/2oz white chocolate drops
Purple food gel
Edible flower petals

1   Preheat the oven to 180°C (160°C fan oven) Gas 4. Grease the Bundt tin with melted butter and dust with a little flour.

2   Cream the butter and sugar together until light and fluffy, and add the eggs one at a time, alternating with the flour. Add the baking powder and ground almonds and briefly mix. Add the almond extract, vanilla and enough milk to loosen the mix.

3   Put half the mixture in another bowl and stir in a little purple food colouring.

4   Spoon the batter into the tin, alternating the plain and purple mixtures. Drag a skewer through the mix a little to create a marble effect.

5   Bake for 35–45 minutes or until a skewer comes out clean. Leave the cake to cool in the tin for 10 minutes, then turn out gently onto a cooling rack and leave to cool completely.

6   To make the ganache, heat the cream in a small saucepan until steaming, then add in the chocolate drops and mix until melted. Leave it to thicken slightly and then pour all over the cake.

7   To decorate, melt the white chocolate in the microwave in 30-second bursts and drizzle some over the cake using a spoon or small piping bag. Add a little purple food gel to the remaining chocolate and drizzle this over in the same way. Add a few edible petals for a pop of colour.

Tip
I place the cake on a cooling rack above a bowl to flood with ganache, spooning over the chocolate as it drips down for a thick, even layer of ganache.

Festive meringue wreath

YOU WILL NEED A BAKING SHEET & A LARGE ROASTING DISH

————

I love this meringue wreath as it serves twelve perfectly sized portions ideal
for celebrations, get-togethers or as dessert when we have family or friends over.
Not only does it look super impressive, the plump roasted fruits in honey,
rum and bay create a delicious topping to make this a guaranteed winner!

SERVES 12

For the meringue
5 large egg whites
285g/10oz caster sugar
1 tsp vanilla bean paste

For the topping
4 plums
150g/5oz/small punnet
    of blackberries
3 bay leaves
30g/1oz pistachios
2 tbsp soft brown sugar
4 tbsp honey
4 tbsp rum (optional)

400ml/14fl oz double cream
4 fresh figs
Handful of redcurrants
Edible flowers, to decorate

1 Heat the oven to 140°C (120°C fan oven) Gas 1. Draw a circle
on baking paper measuring approximately 28cm/11in in diameter,
flip the paper over so the ink side is underneath and place on a
baking sheet.

2 Whisk the egg whites in a bowl or stand mixer until they form
soft peaks, then add the sugar a spoonful at a time. Whisk until
the meringue is shiny and glossy and you can't feel any sugar
grains when you rub a little of the mixture between your fingers.
Add the vanilla, mix well, then use a little of the mixture to secure
the baking paper to the baking sheet on all four corners.

3 Spoon 12 mounds of meringue inside the circle and make
a divot in each mound with the back of a spoon.

4 Bake for 1hr 15mins – 1hr 30mins and leave to cool. The
meringue should be dry to touch on the outside and can peel
away easily from the paper. Leave to cool in the oven for a couple
of hours.

5 For the filling, preheat the oven to 220°C (200°C fan oven)
Gas 7.

6 Quarter the plums and put them in a roasting dish with the
blackberries in a single layer. Tear the bay leaves up and scatter
around the fruits. Add the nuts, sprinkle with the sugar and
drizzle honey and rum over everything. Roast in the oven for
15–20 mins until the fruits are just soft and the juice is thick and
syrupy. Leave to cool completely.

7 To assemble, place the meringue on a large plate. Whip the
double cream until pillowy and slice the figs in half. Spoon the
cream over the meringue and arrange the fruit on top along with
the pistachios and redcurrants. Spoon the syrupy mixture all over
the top and decorate with edible petals.

Tip
Make sure you allow the fruits to
cool completely before assembling
or it will create a soupy, creamy
mess!

Brie en croûte with cranberry

YOU WILL NEED A BAKING SHEET

Cheese night in our house isn't complete unless we have this as a centrepiece on the table. The gooey, creamy brie is encased in buttery pastry topped with sweet and sharp cranberries, and fragrant rosemary adds so much flavour. Serve with an assortment of crackers and bread for dipping and scooping up the melted cheese.

SERVES 4

4 sprigs of fresh rosemary
3 tbsp cranberry sauce
1 tbsp honey
Rough puff pastry (see p.62) or
   1 sheet of ready-rolled puff pastry
Brie wheel (approximately
   470g/1 lb)
2 garlic cloves
Milk, to glaze
Handful of fresh cranberries
Few pecans

1 Finely chop two sprigs of rosemary and mix in a bowl with the cranberry sauce and honey.

2 Roll out the pastry to a square that is larger than the brie wheel, or unroll the pastry sheet; place the brie in the centre and cut a circular shape larger than the brie.

3 Preheat the oven to 220°C (200°C fan oven) Gas 7.

4 Make a few cuts in the top of the brie. Lightly crush the garlic cloves and push them into the cuts. Poke the remaining rosemary sprigs in too.

5 Fold the pastry up the sides of the brie, overlapping the dough as you go. Glaze the pastry with a little milk, then top with the fresh cranberries and half the cranberry sauce mix.

6 Bake for 25–30 minutes until lightly golden, then top with the remaining cranberry sauce. Scatter over some pecans and serve immediately.

Tip
Once baked, serve immediately so the cheese is extra melty. If it hardens, pop in the microwave for a few seconds at a time to melt.

Christmas tree stout cupcakes

YOU WILL NEED A 12-HOLE CUPCAKE TIN & PAPER CASES, A PIPING BAG & STAR NOZZLE

Magic happens when you add stout to chocolate cake! It creates a
tangy flavoured sponge which pairs beautifully with the silky cream cheese frosting,
and let's be honest, these couldn't look any more festive.

MAKES 12 CUPCAKES

For the cupcakes
130g/4½oz unsalted butter
125ml/4½fl oz stout
2 large eggs
225g/8oz caster sugar
80ml/3fl oz buttermilk
1 tsp vanilla bean paste
70g/2½oz cocoa powder
150g/5oz plain flour
1 tsp bicarbonate of soda

For the cream cheese frosting
180g/6½oz unsalted butter
180g/6½oz full fat cream cheese
380g/13½oz icing sugar
Green food gel

To decorate
Fondant icing or ready-made
    fondant stars
Coloured pearls
Icing sugar, to dust

1 Preheat the oven to 180°C (160°C fan oven) Gas 4 and line the cupcake tin with paper cases.

2 Heat the butter and stout together in a small pan until the butter has melted, and leave to cool.

3 Whisk the eggs, sugar, buttermilk and vanilla together in a bowl with the cocoa powder.

4 Add the buttery stout mixture a little at a time and mix well.

5 Sift the flour and bicarbonate of soda over the mixture and mix thoroughly. Divide between the cases and bake for 15–20 minutes until risen or a skewer comes out clean. Leave the cakes to cool on a cooling rack.

6 Dust the worktop with a little icing sugar and roll a little white fondant icing out thinly. Using a star-shape cutter, cut out twelve stars and leave to firm up.

7 For the cream cheese frosting, beat the butter until very soft, add half the cream cheese and beat well. Add the icing sugar and the remaining cream cheese and beat until smooth and creamy. Add a little green food gel, then tip the frosting into a piping bag fitted with a large star nozzle.

8 To assemble, pipe a large star on a cupcake, then two more, reducing the size as you go to resemble a tree.

9 Decorate with coloured pearls and top with a fondant star.

Tip
If the frosting doesn't hold its shape very well, pop it in the fridge to firm up a little, or refrigerate as you pipe each star so they are a little firmer.

Linzer cookies

YOU WILL NEED 2 BAKING SHEETS, A 6CM/2IN COOKIE CUTTER
& A SMALL COOKIE CUTTER

———

Whip up a batch of these buttery melt-in-the-mouth sandwich cookies for your
Christmas table. The tart, tangy jam pairs wonderfully well with the sweet biscuits.

MAKES 12 COOKIES

For the cookies

140g/5oz ground almonds
280g/10oz plain flour
½ tsp ground cinnamon
Large pinch of ground cloves
¼ tsp ground ginger
Large pinch of ground nutmeg
180g/6½oz unsalted butter
100g/2½oz soft brown sugar
2 medium eggs, beaten
1 tsp vanilla bean paste
Zest of 1 orange

Icing sugar, to dust

For the jam filling

12 tsp Cranberry, Apple and
Orange Jam (see p.185)

1 Put the ground almonds, flour, cinnamon, cloves, ginger and
nutmeg in a bowl and roughly mix.

2 Cream the butter and sugar together until light and fluffy then
add half the beaten egg, the vanilla and zest and mix well. Add the
dry ingredients and the remaining egg and beat until it comes
together in a rough ball.

3 Flatten the dough into a disc shape, wrap in baking parchment
and pop into the fridge to firm up.

4 Preheat the oven to 180°C (160°C fan oven) Gas 4 and line
two baking sheets with parchment.

5 Divide the chilled dough in half. Roll one piece to about 3mm
thick and stamp out 12 cookies using a 6cm cutter, placing them
onto one of the baking sheets. Repeat with the second piece of
dough in the same way, but this time stamp out little shapes with
a small cutter from the other 12 cookies.

6 Pop the trays in the fridge to firm up for around 15 minutes,
then bake for 8–10 minutes. The cookies should be pale in colour.
Mix the jam to loosen, then spoon a teaspoon on each of the plain
cookies. Top with the other cookies with the cut-out shapes and
dust with a little icing sugar.

Tip
If the dough is a little sticky, pop it
in the fridge to harden slightly or
roll between two sheets of baking
parchment.

Christmas cake

YOU WILL NEED 2 X 15CM/6IN ROUND LOOSE-BOTTOMED CAKE TINS

I'm not sure about you, but with all the overindulging we do over Christmas,
we're always left with Christmas cake going into the New Year.
This recipe makes the perfect amount for two smaller cakes – one for you and
one for a friend. Spread the love this Christmas.

EACH CAKE SERVES 12

For the cakes

300g/10½oz sultanas
150g/5oz currants
150g/5oz raisins
100g/3½oz dried apricots
200g/7oz cranberries
50g/1½oz glacé cherries
50g/1½oz mixed peel
Zest and juice of 1 orange
170ml/6fl oz sherry
250g/9oz unsalted butter,
    plus extra for greasing
250g/9oz soft brown sugar
1½ tsp vanilla bean paste
4 large eggs
220g/7½oz plain flour
1½ tsp ground mixed spice
120g/4oz nuts, I use a mix of pecans,
    almonds and Brazil nuts

To decorate

Apricot jam
Pack of ready-to-roll marzipan
Pack of ready-to-roll white icing
Icing sugar, to dust

1 Chop all the larger dried fruit and add to a bowl with the smaller fruits. Add the orange juice, zest and alcohol, then mix well and cover with a clean tea towel overnight to plump up.

2 The following day, grease and double line the cake tins, and wrap the outside of the tins with newspaper secured with string.

3 Preheat the oven to 160°C (140°C fan oven) Gas 3.

4 Beat the butter, sugar, vanilla and eggs together, then add the flour and mixed spice and thoroughly mix. Add the fruits and any liquid from the bowl, mix in the chopped nuts then divide equally between the two tins. Level the tops with a spatula and bake for 1½ hours.

5 Reduce the heat to 140°C (120°C fan oven) Gas 1 and bake for a further 1–1¼ hours until baked, or check with a skewer.

6 Leave the cakes to cool completely in the tins, then wrap in foil and store in the cupboard until ready to decorate. If you want to feed your cake in the lead-up to Christmas, unwrap the cake, poke holes all over the top with a cocktail stick and drizzle with your chosen alcohol.

7 I decorate my Christmas cakes a week before eating, by warming a little apricot jam and brushing a thin layer on the top and sides of the cake. Roll out the marzipan on a worktop lightly dusted with icing sugar and, using the rolling pin to help, lift the marzipan onto the cake, smoothing the top and sides. Repeat with the rolled fondant icing and decorate the cake as you wish.

Tip
If the tops of the cakes are browning too quickly, cover them loosely with foil.

Smokey pulled pork sausage rolls

YOU WILL NEED A SLOW COOKER & A BAKING SHEET

————

We hate waste as a family so I always make sure I use up leftovers. I cook pork in the slow cooker during the day and serve it in delicious crusty rolls with a homemade coleslaw that evening for a winter warmer. When we have some pork left over, I love making a batch of these smokey sausage rolls for lunch the following day.

MAKES 8

Sausage rolls
Rough puff pastry (see p.62)
    or 1 sheet ready-rolled puff pastry
1 medium egg
Dried chilli flakes

For the pulled pork
2kg/4 lb 4oz pork shoulder
    (rind and fat removed)
40g/1½oz soft dark brown sugar
4 tbsp smoked paprika
1 tbsp cayenne pepper
1 tbsp ground cumin
1 tsp pepper
1 tsp sea salt
1 tbsp dry mustard powder
2 tsp thyme
340ml/12fl oz water
200ml/7fl oz barbecue sauce

1 For the pork, remove the rind and fat and place in a large dish.

2 In a small bowl mix together the sugar, paprika, cayenne, cumin, pepper, salt, mustard powder and thyme. Scatter the dry rub all over the pork, coating it on both sides, cover and place in the fridge overnight.

3 The following day, place the pork into the slow cooker with the water and let it cook, checking the manufacturer's instructions as the cooking time is dependent on your slow cooker. Mine cooks on low in around 6 hours, and pulls apart easily when pressed with two forks.

4 Shred the pork with two forks and place into a dish. Skim the fat off the surface of the juices in the slow cooker. Using a ladle, remove some of the liquid and mix with the barbecue sauce. Add more juices from the slow cooker and serve.

5 Place the leftover meat in the fridge in a bowl covered with cling film.

6 To make the sausage rolls, preheat the oven to 220°C (200°C fan oven) Gas 7. Unroll the pastry sheet (or if using your own rough puff, roll out to 23 x 35cm/9 x 14in), then cut into eight equal pieces.

7 Remove the pork from the fridge and divide into eight pieces. Roll each piece into a sausage shape, the same width as the pastry, and roll up. Crimp the edge or press with a fork to seal.

8 Beat the egg and egg wash each pork roll. Sprinkle a few dried chilli flakes on each one.

9 Bake for 20 minutes until the pastry is golden brown.

Tip
By leaving the pork to marinate overnight the meat absorbs the spices to give a real depth of flavour.

Ginger & cranberry cupcake wreath

YOU WILL NEED A 12-HOLE CUPCAKE TIN & PAPER CASES, A PIPING BAG & STAR NOZZLE,
A STAR CUTTER & A PINECONE MOULD (OPTIONAL)

These sticky ginger cupcakes are full of warming spices and tart fresh cranberries. Shaping the finished cupcakes into a wreath makes them the perfect Christmas centrepiece for sharing. So easy to assemble but it looks so impressive!

MAKES 12

For the cupcakes

125g/4½oz unsalted butter
170g/6oz dark muscovado sugar
150g/5oz golden syrup
270g/9½oz plain flour
¾ tsp bicarbonate of soda
1½ tsp ground ginger
1 tsp ground cinnamon
2 large eggs, beaten
100ml/3½fl oz buttermilk
2 balls of stem ginger, chopped
100g/3½oz fresh cranberries

For the cream cheese frosting

180g/6½oz unsalted butter
380g/13½oz icing sugar
180g/6½oz full fat cream cheese
1 tsp vanilla bean paste

To decorate

White fondant
Brown fondant
Few frozen cranberries
Meringue kisses
  (optional, see p.79)

Tip

If you don't have a pinecone mould, simply roll a piece of brown fondant into a cone shape and flatten slightly. Using a small pair of scissors, snip the base of the cone to create little points. Work all the way around then up to the top, teasing the ends up gently to create texture. Leave to dry.

1 Preheat your oven to 170°C (150°C fan oven) Gas 3 and line a cupcake tin with paper cases.

2 Put the butter, sugar and golden syrup into a small saucepan, and heat gently until the butter has melted. Leave to cool.

3 Sift the flour, bicarbonate of soda, ground ginger and cinnamon into a bowl. Add the buttery mixture, along with the beaten eggs, buttermilk and chopped stem ginger.

4 Stir through the cranberries and pour the mixture into the paper cases. Bake for about 20–25 minutes until golden. These cupcakes won't rise much as they are fairly dense and sticky.

5 Leave the cupcakes to cool completely in the tin, then move onto a cooling rack while you make the frosting.

6 To make the decorations, roll out the white fondant and cut out a few stars. Press some brown fondant into a pinecone mould and leave to harden.

7 For the cream cheese frosting, beat the butter until light and soft and add the icing sugar. Beat well, then add the cream cheese and vanilla and continue to mix until smooth.

8 To assemble, arrange the cupcakes in a wreath shape. Snip the end off a piping bag and push a star-shaped piping nozzle into the end. Fill the bag with the frosting and pipe a large swirl on top of each cupcake, starting in the middle and working outwards, keeping it level.

9 Top with frozen cranberries, meringue kisses and the fondant stars and pinecones.

When we have a glut of fruit

from the garden, I often freeze it to use throughout the year,
but one of my great loves is jam. It's great in sandwiches, on toast,
in cakes and so much more. Jam is so easy to make and jars are
perfect to give as little gifts to friends and family.

Here are some of my top tips for successful jam

- I tend to use jam sugar because it contains added pectin, which helps jams set and keep their colour and flavour.

- To sterilise jam jars, wash them in warm soapy water and preheat your oven to 120°C (100°C fan oven) Gas ½. Place the jars in the oven on a baking sheet and leave until completely dry.

- To check if the jam is ready, I spoon a little amount onto a plate that's been in the freezer. If the jam ripples, it's ready to spoon into the jars and screw on lids tightly. Alternatively you can use a jam thermometer.

- Label your jars and store them in a cool dark place. Once opened, pop in the fridge.

- Depending on the size of your jars, these recipes make 1–2 full jars.

Rhubarb & raspberry jam

———

200g/7oz rhubarb
200g/7oz raspberries
400g/14oz jam sugar
Juice of ½ lemon

1 Chop the rhubarb into 2.5cm/1in pieces and put in a heavy-based saucepan along with the raspberries.

2 Add the sugar and lemon juice and heat over a medium heat until the sugar has dissolved, then turn up the heat and allow the fruits to boil.

3 Test the jam by spooning a small amount onto a plate that has been in the freezer. Drag your finger through the jam: if it wrinkles, it's ready. Spoon into the sterilised jars or use a jam funnel, screw on the lids and label.

Raspberry & rose jam

———

400g/14oz raspberries
400g/14oz jam sugar
Juice of ½ lemon
1 tsp rose water

1 Mash the raspberries in a heavy-based saucepan and add the sugar and lemon juice. Heat over a medium heat until the sugar has dissolved, then turn up the heat and allow the fruits to boil.

2 Test the jam by spooning a small amount onto a plate that has been in the freezer. Drag your finger through the jam: if it wrinkles, it's ready. Stir the rose water into the jam then spoon into the sterilised jars, screw on the lids and label.

Strawberry & vanilla jam

———

400g/14oz strawberries
400g/14oz jam sugar
Juice of ½ lemon
1 tsp vanilla bean paste

1 Hull the fruit by cutting a cone shape into the top of each strawberry to remove the stem. Quarter the fruit, then add to a heavy-based saucepan and add the sugar and lemon juice. Heat over a medium heat until the sugar has dissolved, then turn up the heat and allow the fruits to boil.

2 Test the jam by spooning a small amount onto a plate that has been in the freezer. Drag your finger through the jam: if it wrinkles, it's ready. Stir the vanilla into the jam then spoon into the sterilised jars, screw on the lids and label.

Pear & ginger jam

400g/14oz pears
1 ball of stem ginger
400g/14oz jam sugar
Juice of ½ lemon

1   Peel, core and chop the pears and place in a heavy-based saucepan. Finely chop the ginger and add to the saucepan along with the sugar and lemon juice. Heat over a medium heat until the sugar has dissolved, then turn up the heat and allow the fruits to boil.

2   Test the jam by spooning a small amount onto a plate that has been in the freezer. Drag your finger through the jam: if it wrinkles, it's ready. Spoon the jam into the sterilised jars, screw on the lids and label.

Blackberry & bay jam

400g/14oz blackberries
400g/14oz jam sugar
Juice of ½ lemon
3 bay leaves

1   Mash the blackberries in a heavy-based saucepan and add the sugar and lemon juice. Add the bay leaves to the pan. Heat over a medium heat until the sugar has dissolved, then turn up the heat and allow the fruits to boil.

2   Test the jam by spooning a small amount onto a plate that has been in the freezer. Drag your finger through the jam: if it wrinkles, it's ready. Remove the bay leaves, then spoon the jam into the sterilised jars, screw on the lids and label.

Cranberry, apple & orange jam

2 eating apples
300g/10½oz fresh cranberries
2 oranges
450g/1 lb jam sugar
Juice of ½ lemon
180ml/6fl oz pomegranate juice

1   Peel, core and roughly chop the apples and add to a food processor. Add the cranberries and the zest of the oranges. Peel and remove the pith from the oranges and add the flesh to the food processor. Blitz all the ingredients then put them in a heavy-based saucepan along with the sugar, lemon juice and pomegranate juice.

2   Heat over a medium heat for the sugar to dissolve, then turn up the heat and bubble to thicken. Test the jam by spooning a small amount onto a plate that has been in the freezer. Drag your finger through the jam: if it wrinkles, it's ready. Spoon the jam into the sterilised jars, screw on the lids and label.

Lemon & lime curd

1 lemon
1 lime
50g/1½oz unsalted butter
80g/3oz caster sugar
1 egg
1 egg yolk

1 Zest and juice the lemon and lime into a heavy-based pan. Add all the other ingredients and whisk together well. Heat over a low heat until all the butter has melted.

2 Turn up the heat to medium and continue to whisk for 8–10 minutes until the curd is thick enough to coat the back of a spoon.

3 Spoon into a sterilised jar, screw on the lid and label. Once cooled, keep in the fridge and use within a week or two.

Seville orange curd

4 Seville oranges
100g/3½oz unsalted butter
150g/5oz caster sugar
2 eggs
2 egg yolks

1 Zest and juice the oranges and put in a heavy-based pan. Add all the other ingredients and whisk together well.

2 Heat over a low heat until all the butter has melted. Turn up the heat to medium and continue to whisk for 8–10 minutes until the curd is thick enough to coat the back of a spoon.

3 Spoon into sterilised jars, screw on lids and label. Once cooled, keep in the fridge and use within a week or two.

Acknowledgements

Wow! I can't believe I'm writing this! Writing a book takes a lot of time, effort and hard work, but I'm so very grateful and lucky to have been given the chance to turn a dream into a reality.

I want to say a massive thank you to you, for going out to buy this book. I hope you enjoy baking through this book with me, and that these bakes become family favourites in your home as they have in mine.

A huge thank you to my amazing family for all your love and the support you show me. I couldn't have done it without you all.

To my Dad and Mam, for teaching me the basics of cooking, baking and gardening from such an early age and for just being you! I hope I've made you proud.

To my sister Nerys, for always being at the end of the phone when I needed you and for those FaceTime calls with little Felix to brighten up my day.

Emilia, keep baking with Teresa, especially your delicious chocolate cake!

To Kath, for sticking by me – I'm so grateful for our friendship and looking forward to our boys continuing to be there for each other as we have all these years.

Thanks to my chief taste-testers, Uncle Kevin and Auntie Veronica, who ate their way through all the test bakes during lockdown, and for always letting me know what their favourites were.

To Ben, my husband (aka food photographer and food stylist). Thanks for turning your hand to being the best photographer I could ever have wished for. The beautiful photos in this book have been lovingly taken by you and there's no one else I'd rather have worked with on this book. The book is something special to have come out of lockdown, a real team effort, but months of being stuck at home has resulted in something amazing. We will both look back through these recipes and photos and be reminded of those precious months we spent making memories as a family. Those late nights and expanding waistlines were worth it! We have always been, and always will be, an 'effective team'.

Thanks to all the amazing people at Love Productions for fulfilling my dream of baking in the big white tent. I am so grateful you gave me the opportunity and for giving me the platform to follow this path with my love for baking. The whole experience was an unforgettable and surreal one made better by the other twelve amazing bakers.

A big thank you to the fabulous team at Northbank Talent for believing in me from the beginning. Thanks to Martin for getting my book idea off the ground and for giving me the confidence to do it. Thanks to Lorna and Rob for being such great agents, always keeping me busy with fantastic work opportunities, and for keeping me on track.

Thanks to my great publishers and editors at Little, Brown for loving my book idea as much as me, and to Tom and Andrew for all your amazing work and making this book look and feel so very special.

Finally, to my two boys, Ben and Alfie, for being my rock, my world, my everything. Thanks for all your encouragement, support and for believing in me when times got tough.
I love you both with all my heart forever.

Index